Cree Version

NISTOMITANAW ASKIY NIHTĀTĀPASINAHIKĒWIN

kihci mitātahtomitanaw, kēkā-mitātahtwāw mitātahtomitanaw, kētā-mitātahtomitanaw nīsosāp – nīswāw kihci-mitātahtomitanaw nīsitanaw nīsosāp

30 Years of Fine Arts 1992-2022

NĒHIYAWI NIKAMOWINA, NĪMIHITOWINA, TĀPASINAHIKĒWINA MĪNA ĀCIMOWINA IYINITO-AYISIYINĪWIWINAK Ē-MIYOWĀTAHKIK PĪKISKWĒWINA

CELEBRATING INDIGENOUS LANGUAGES THROUGH SONG, DANCE, ART, AND STORIES

Translated by Leona Peters-Munroe

Published by:
Big Moose Publishing
Box 127 Site 601 RR#6
Saskatoon, SK S7K 3J9
www.bigmoosepublishing.com

Front Cover Art Credit: North Star Screen Printing
ISBN: 978-1-989840-53-5

Big Moose Publishing 06/2023

This book is dedicated to the memory of Larry Goldade, and to all the Chiefs and communities of the Prince Albert Grand Council.

PAGC CHIEF'S ACT 2015

The Prince Albert Grand Council Executive will provide leadership in a comprehensive way to address issues of common concern that affect PAGC First Nation communities and its members, including treaty protection, resource development, and revenue sharing.

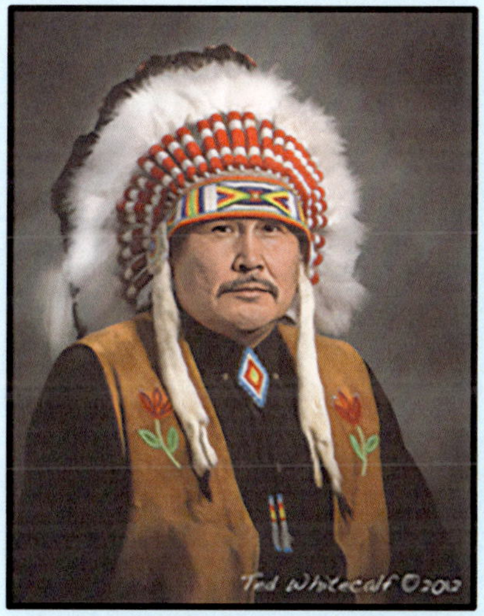

Grand Chief Brian Hardlotte, member of Lac La Ronge Indian Band, was elected in October 2017 and is serving his 2nd term as Grand Chief.

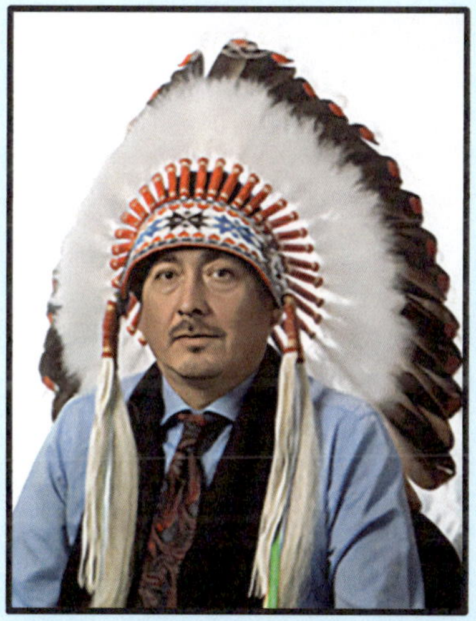

Vice Chief Joseph Tsannie, member of the Hatchet Lake Denesuline First Nation; was re-elected in October 2015 and is serving his 3rd term as Vice Chief.

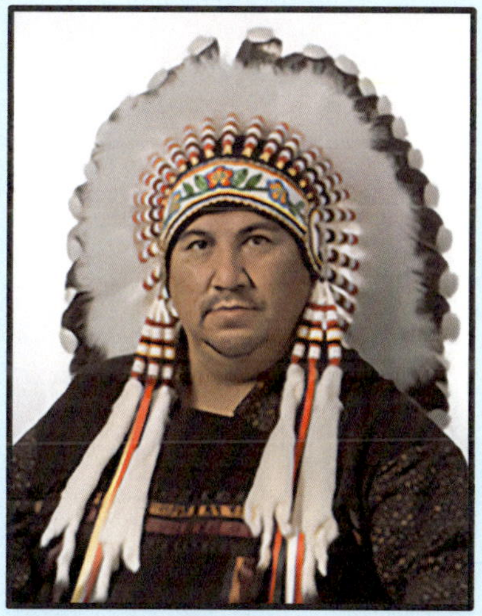

Vice Chief Christopher Jobb, member of Peter Ballantyne Cree Nation; was elected in October 2016 and is serving his 2nd term as Vice Chief.

IN MEMORIAM

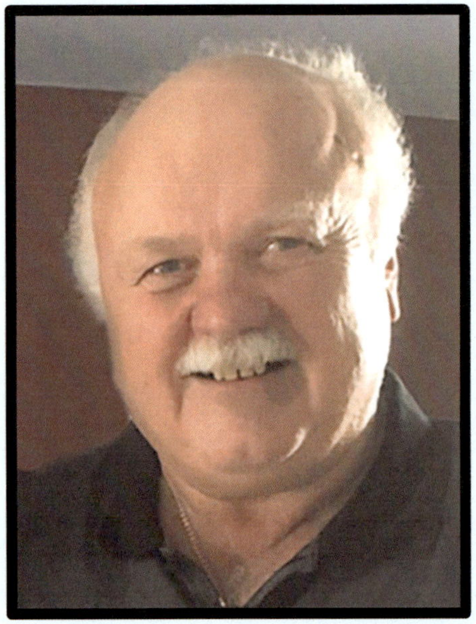

Larry Goldade
1948-2020

In 1990, the idea of hosting an event that was specific to First Nations students who were artistically inclined was being tossed around within the Prince Albert Grand Council. It was a Teacher Services Consultant, by the name of Derroll Leblanc, who thought that there was a need to host such an event. Furthermore, there was no place in Saskatchewan hosting a non-sporting event made specific for First Nations students. By 1991, the idea of the Fine Arts Festival blossomed into a reality. The Prince Albert District Chiefs (known as PAGC) welcomed 200 students and chaperones to Prince Albert where they showcased their artistic and performing talents.

Larry Goldade was the driving force behind the festival because he knew our students were worthy of such an amazing event. He once said, “Not everyone is a hockey player, soccer player, or baseball player. There needs to be something for those students who are not into sports." Thirty years later, PAGC continues to host 1800-2000 participants annually, made up of students, chaperones, and their families to the Fine Arts Festival. All PAGC schools, teachers, and students begin preparing for the festival in September or October, and look forward to it every year.

Larry always advocated for the festival; he believed that there should be something special for every child; especially those who were not athletes. Everyone has a special gift – whether it be sports, academic ability, or creativity for the arts. Every child should be able to shine and that is what this festival is about –giving all students at all ages the opportunity to shine at something that they love to do. The festival was something that Larry was very proud of and he always bragged that we were the only tribal council in the country that does this; others have tried, but have not had the success that we have.

IN MEMORIAM

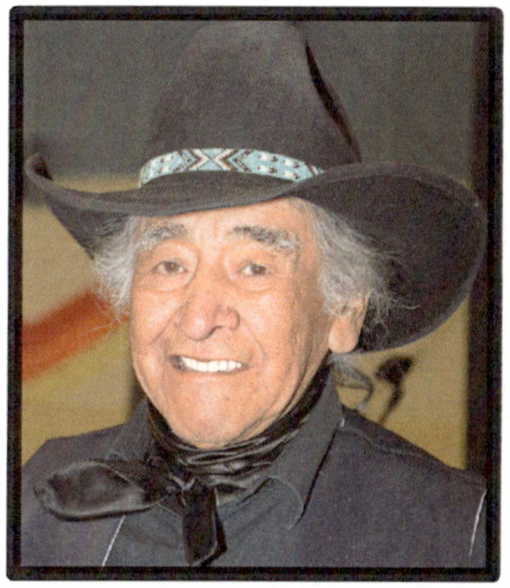

Howard Walker
1944-2022

Howard Walker January 8, 1944 – March 11, 2022 – Howard Walker was a respected Elder, friend and very well known for his presence as MC for many Pow Wows, gatherings, and events. Howard was MC for the Fine Arts Festival for at least 24 years. He had a way of keeping the crowd engaged with the event by telling his jokes and keeping them entertained. At the festival he would always refer to himself as "MOOSHUM" to the audience and the participants. During the Grand Entry, Howard would talk about the veterans that fought in the wars and the flags and their meanings. While the Pow Wow exhibition danced, he would take the time to talk about the different styles of dance and would make sure and let everyone know to "DANCE YOUR STYLE".

He spoke with a reporter at PA Now in 2016 and this is how he summed up his life. "I wouldn't want to change anything. I've got my partner, I've got my grandchildren, and I've got this job. To me, all my children are alive, they're all professionals. Somebody is looking after me up there to be this lucky. Perhaps it's the job that I do, maybe I earned something; because I give so much, I give so much from here," Walker said, gesturing to his heart.

Florence Elaine Walker September 19, 1965 – March 11, 2022 – Elaine and Howard came as a set; you can't have one without the other, that's the way they both wanted it. She took part in the pipe ceremonies and was by Howard's side when he was performing his duties as MC. If he needed something, she was right there to make sure it happened.

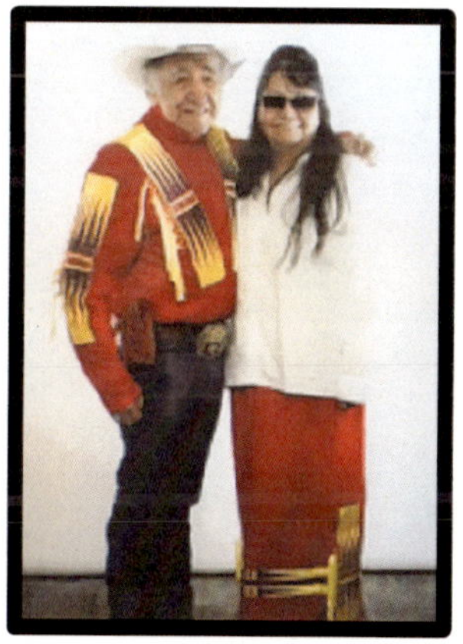

Howard Walker with his wife Elaine.

Howard and Elaine were such big supporters of the festival that he always made sure to contact the Coordinator for dates before he was booked up for the pow wow season. Both were and are loved; and are so very missed. Thoughts turn to Howard and Elaine when Fine Arts Festival time comes around. Fly high with the eagles Howard and Elaine.

Fine Arts Festival Co-ordinator

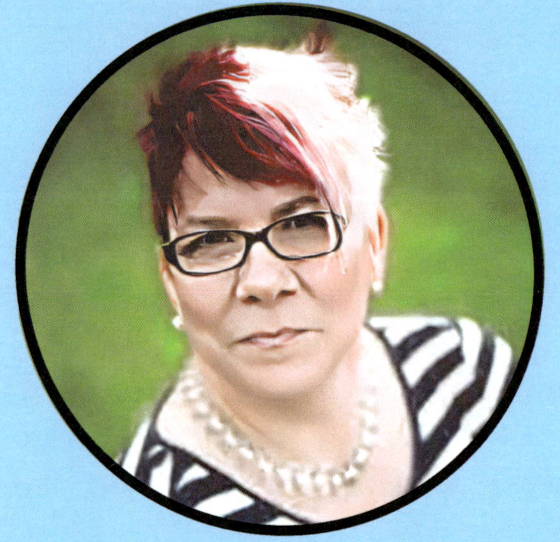

Shona Lee Tretiak started working with PAGC Education in 1993 as a Clerk/Receptionist. She remained in that position for 5 years after which she moved into the Administrative Assistant position and remained in that position for 14 years before she became an RMO Student Files Coordinator until 2019. She now works in the finance department at the main office.

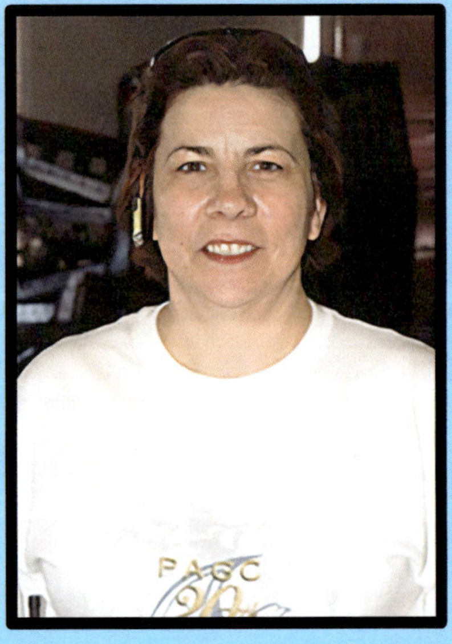

In her 30 year career she has undertaken the task of looking after one of the events through the education office that is directly related to the students – the Fine Arts Festival. She has been the coordinator of the event for the past 29 years. **This year marks her 30th year as the Coordinator of the Fine Arts Festival.**

ABOUT THE AUTHORS

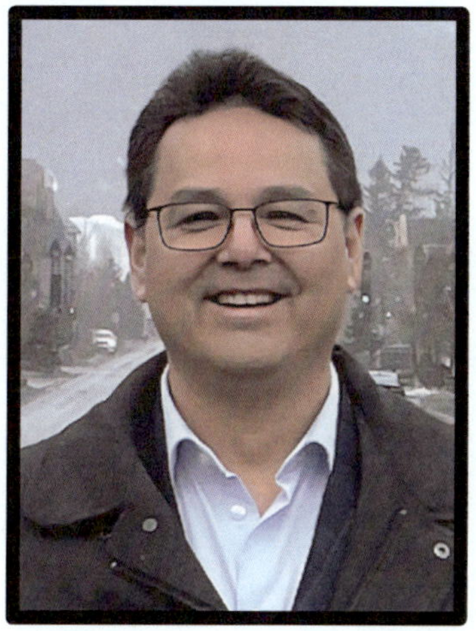

Edward Mirasty, a Lac La Ronge Indian Band Member, is the Director of Education for the Prince Albert Grand Council. He is also in his final year of an Interdisciplinary Ph.D. Program at the University of Saskatchewan. He has been involved in education for over twenty-eight years with most of it at an administration capacity. Our education office has evolved over the past three years to develop more resources that share the rich history, culture and languages of PAGC members. Edward has been happily married for over thirty-one years, and he is the proud father of a little girl named Lilly-B.

Vince Brittain is a James Smith Cree Nation Band member who grew up and attended school at Bernard Constant Community School. He has been married to his wife Connie for over twenty-one years. They have two boys. The eldest, Merit, has completed his second year at the University of Regina in Social Work, and has now entered his first year of Education through the First Nations University of Canada. His youngest, Merik, is attending Grade 12 at Carlton Comprehensive High School. Vince has been involved in education for over 26 years and is currently finishing up his first year of a Doctorate of Education through the University of Saskatchewan. He currently works at the Prince Albert Grand Council as their Third Level Specialist. He believes in honesty, integrity, and trustworthiness, which leads to strong relationships. Vince's parents truly believed in education and strongly supported him in his educational journey. They would be proud of him as he continues with his educational journey and helps empower communities as they move forward.

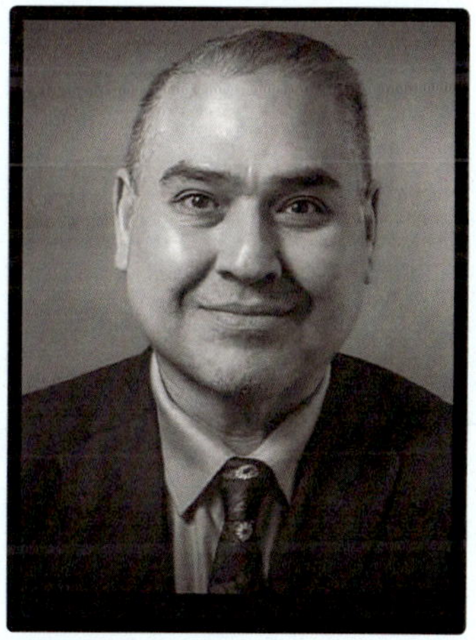

Mandate of the PAGC

The Senior Management Team shall include the Executive Director, the Director of Human Resources, the Director of Finance and such technical, professional or other advisors, specialists or consultants as may be considered necessary to make informed decisions.

The PAGC Senior Management Team

Al Ducharme	Executive Director	Rick Sanderson	Director of Justice
Gene Der	Director of Finance	Geoff Despins	Director of Urban Services
Karen Timmerman	Director of Human Resources	Betty Marleau	Director of Agriculture
Shirley Woods	Director of Health & Social Development	Joan Breland	Director of Holistic Wellness
Frank Bighead	Director of Housing Services	Leona Sorenon	Director of CCEC
Cliff Beuttner	Director of Emergency Services	Mike Wells	Director of IT
Edward Mirasty	Director of Education	Blake Charles	Director of NLCDC
Carol Connolly	Director of Spiritual Healing Lodge		

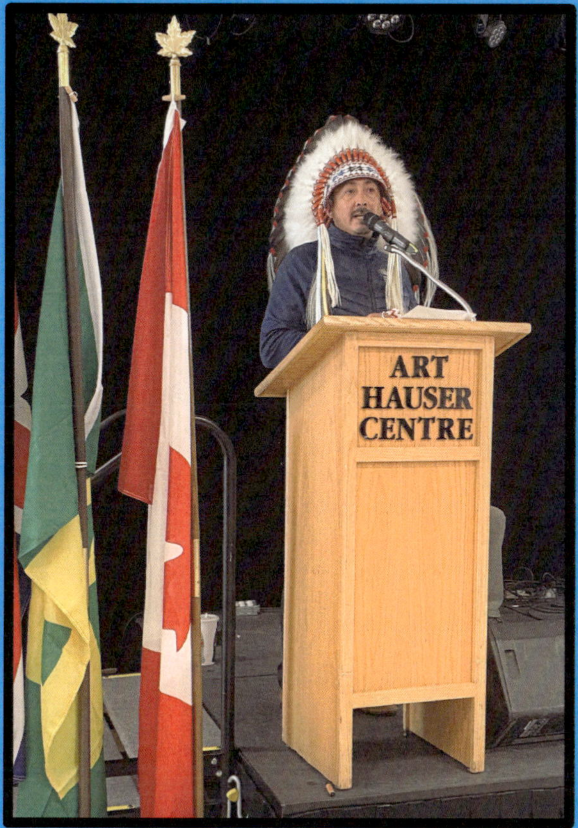

Vice Chief Joseph Tsannie

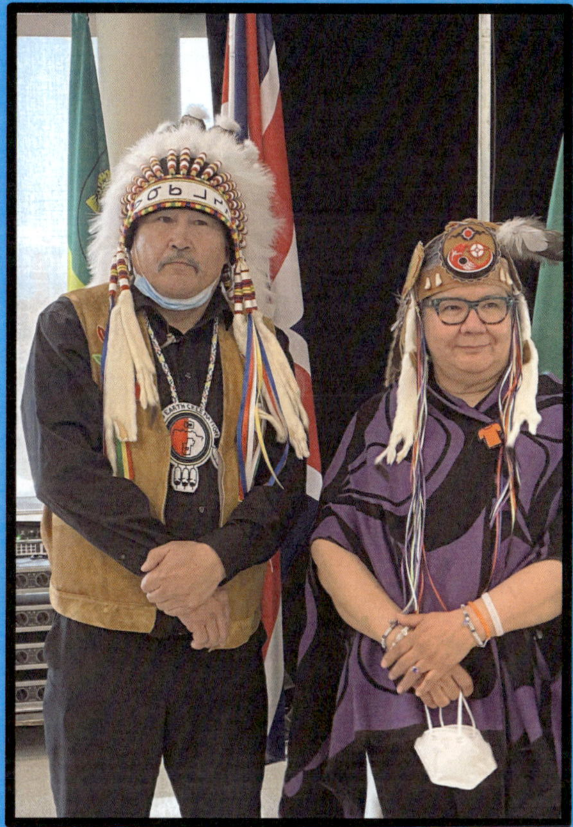

Grand Chief, Brian Hardlotte and Assembly of First Nations Grand Chief, Roseanne Archibald

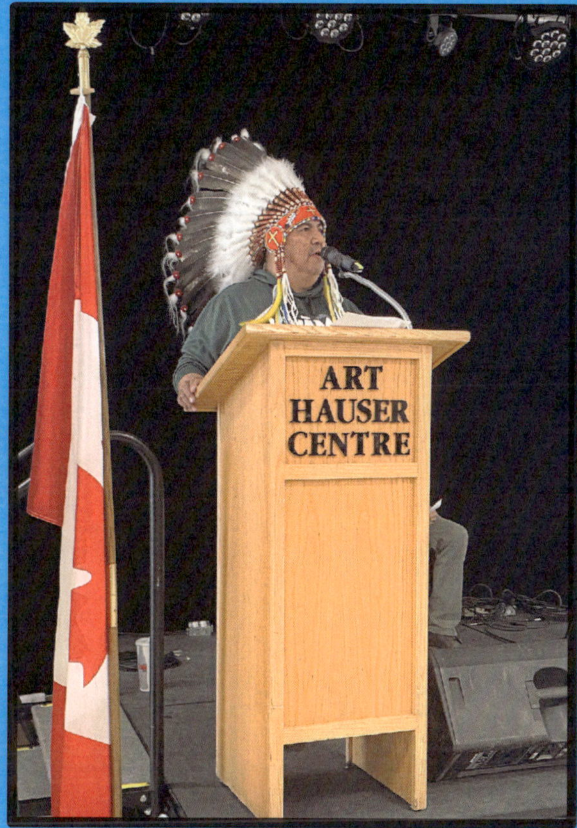

Vice Chief Christopher Jobb

Awasi-sikwanohk kakī-mōcikihtāwinihkēwin kanīpāyamihahk ayiwāk nawac kihci kīkway. Ēyako awa kihci-okimahkāniskwēw Roseanne Archibald ē-kī-wīcihtāsot māmawapowin nīkān tahtoskānēsihk ohci. Kī-sīhkihkēmēw ōhi kapē-māmawipayicik ēkwa mīna ē-kī-wīcī-masinipayitawāt kihci-okimāwa Brian Hardlotta.

Last year's Festival was extra special. In attendance was Assembly of First Nations Grand Chief, Roseanne Archibald. She offered words of encouragement to the attendees and had pictures with Grand Chief, Brian Hardlotte.

Ōma mētawēstamākēw-itōhtēwina kī-pē-itahkamikahk ōtē nēhiyawikiskinwa-hamawākanak ka-māmaskācinākosicik.

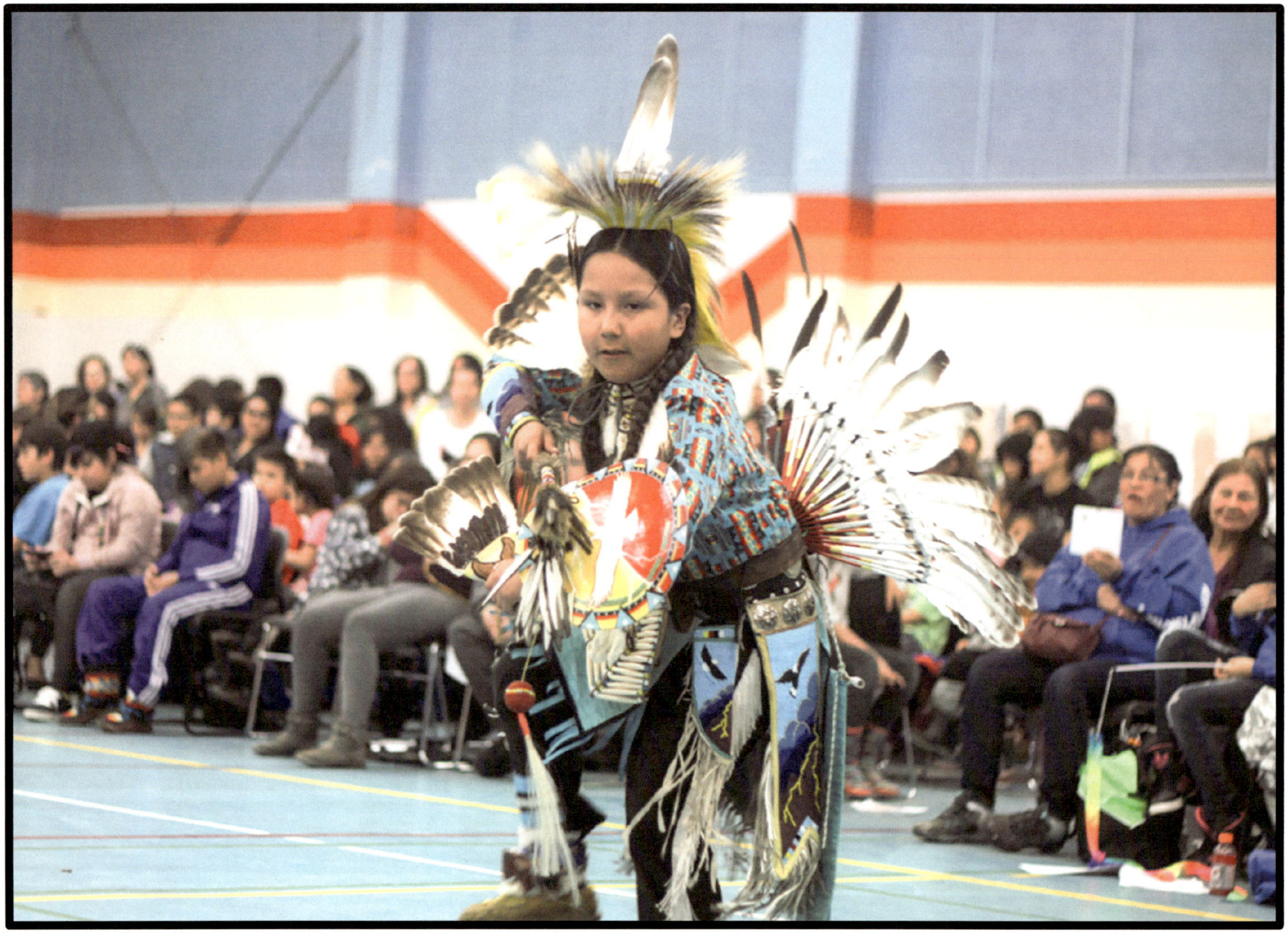

This Festival of Arts has grown to become a showcase for First Nations' students wishing to display a wide range of artistic talent.

Ēkospīhk anima kā-ispayik itahkamikisēwina ōki okiskinwahamawākanak māmawi-isīh-cikēwak, naspasinahikēwina, ācimowina, nīmihtowina, kitohcikēwina, ēkwa mīna ē-kiskinowāpahtihēcik ayiwāk ka-nakacihtācik osīhcikēwinawa.

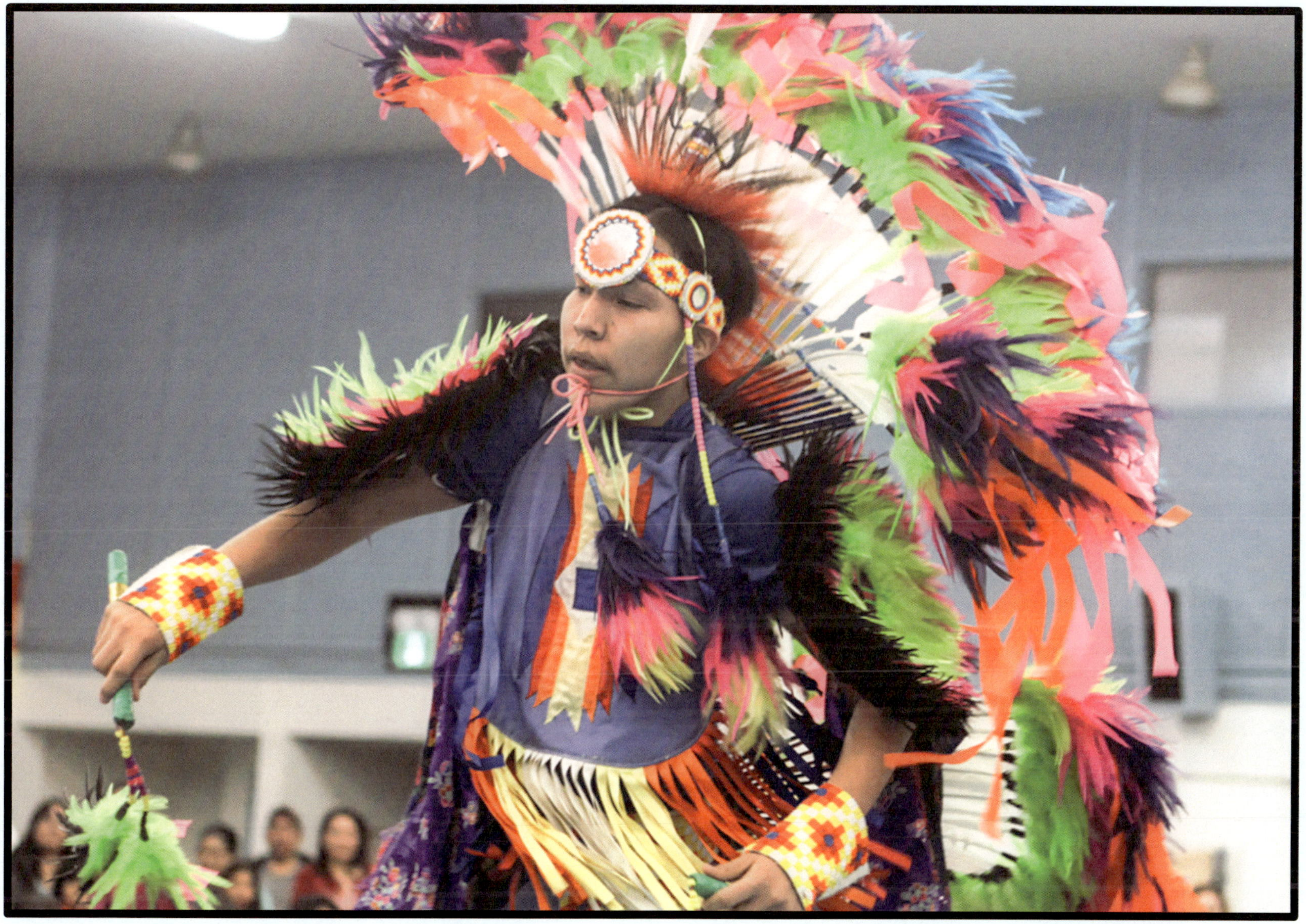

One of the dancers at the PAGC Fine Arts Festival. Arthur White-Crummey/Daily Herald

During this week-long event, students participate in visual arts, drama, dance, music, and literature, and learn hands on skills to enhance their talents.

MUSICAL ARTS

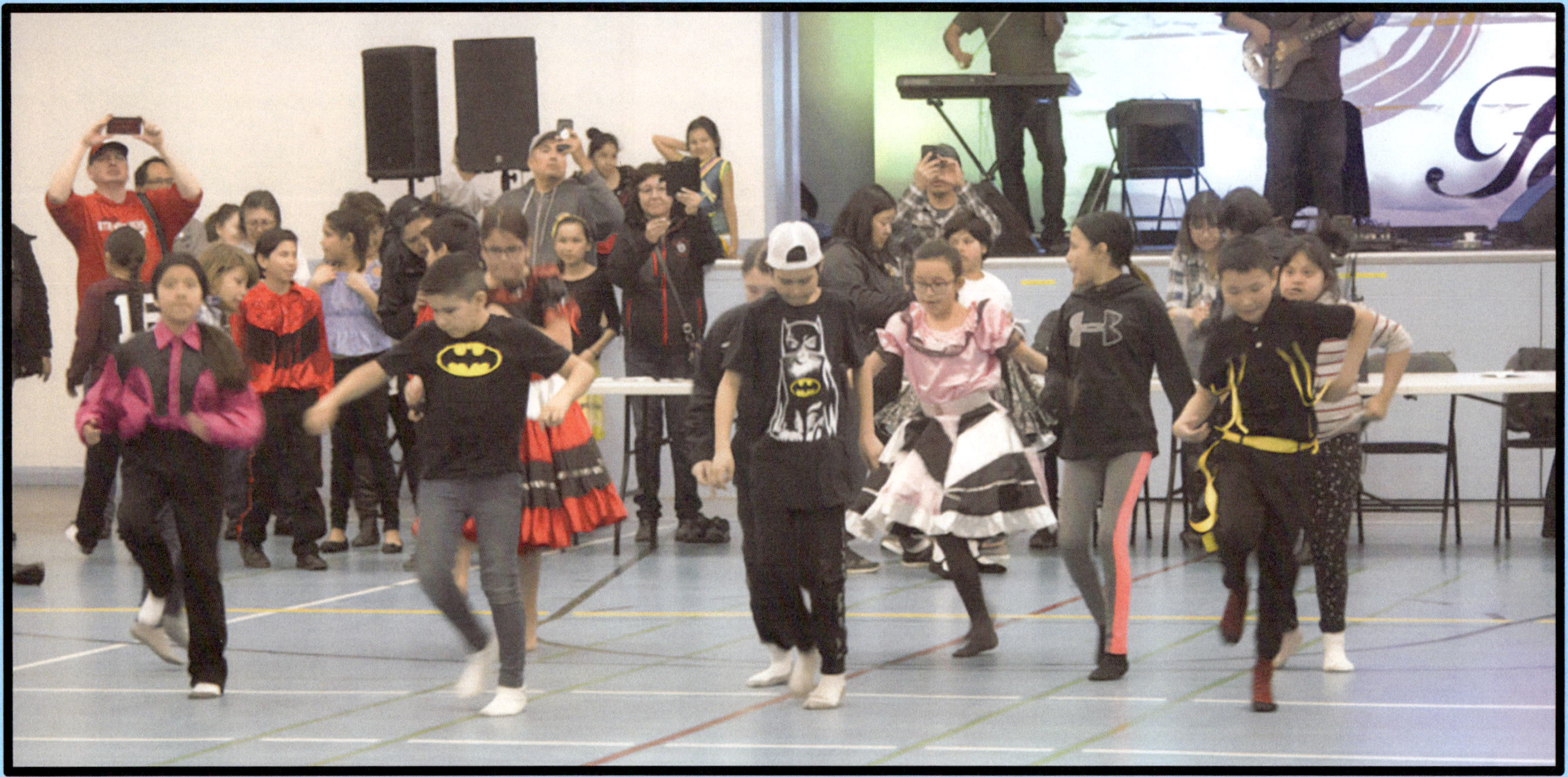

Kiskinwahamawākanak kīwētinohk ohci, ayamihēwiyiniw porte kiskisiwin cīpwayān kiskinwa-hamātowikamik, kaskitēwi-sākahikan ōtē awa corden sayazie ka-ohcīt. Māka ē-kī-pē-nīsosimot kakī-mācihtāk ēkospīhk kamōcikihtāwinihkēhk. Nīsitanaw kēka-mitātahtosāp-āskiy. Kistap-inānihk kihci-wiyasiwēwak ōki kekī-pimipayihtācik.

Students from across the north, including Corden Sayazie (front row, far right) from Father Porte Memorial Dene School in Black Lake, compete in a jigging competition during the opening day of the 2019 PAGC Fine Arts Festival. - Jason Kerr/ Daily Herald

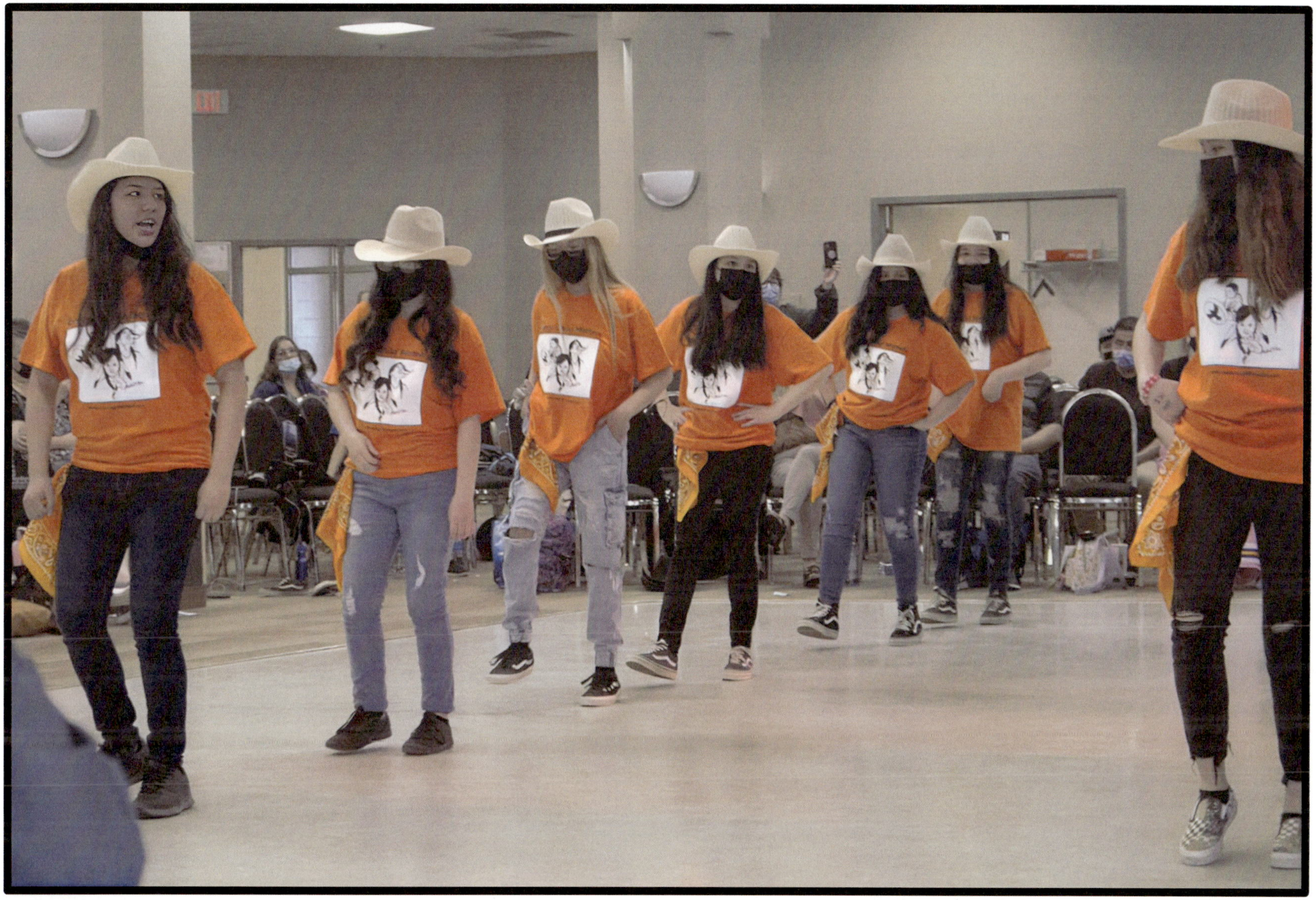

Kiskinwahamawākanak ākōsimowak ēkospīhk ka-māmawi-nīmihtocik ēkotē kistapināni-hk kihci-wiyasiwēwak ka-pimipayihtācik mētawēstamākēwitōhtēwinihk. Opawikoscikan, wapawiksikan kininwahamātowikamik ohci ōki.

Students from Wapawikoscikan School in Pelican Narrows perform a line dance during a group dance competition at the 2022 PAGC Fine Arts Festival.

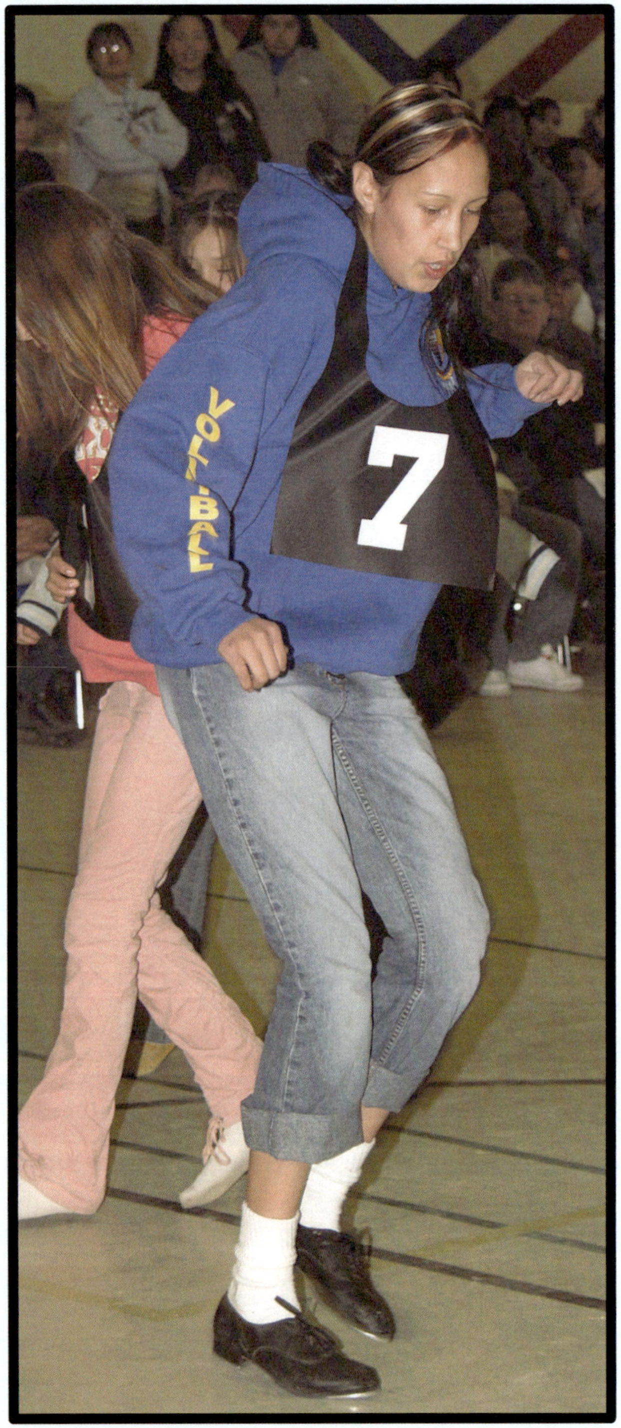
7

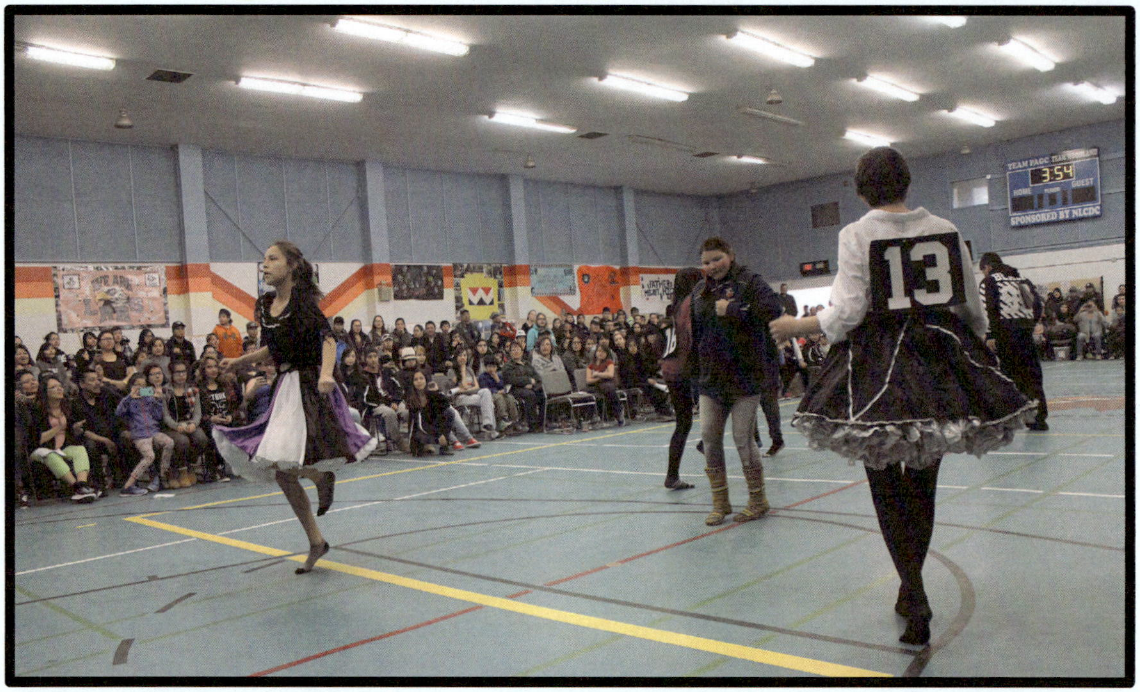
13
SPONSORED BY NLCDC

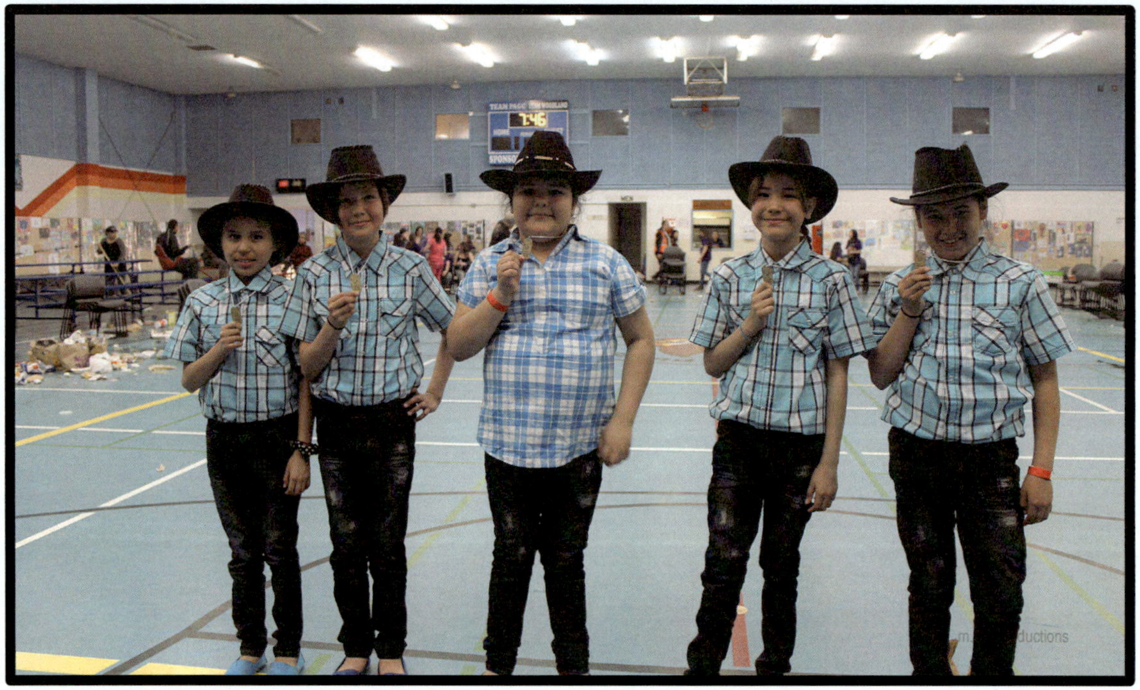

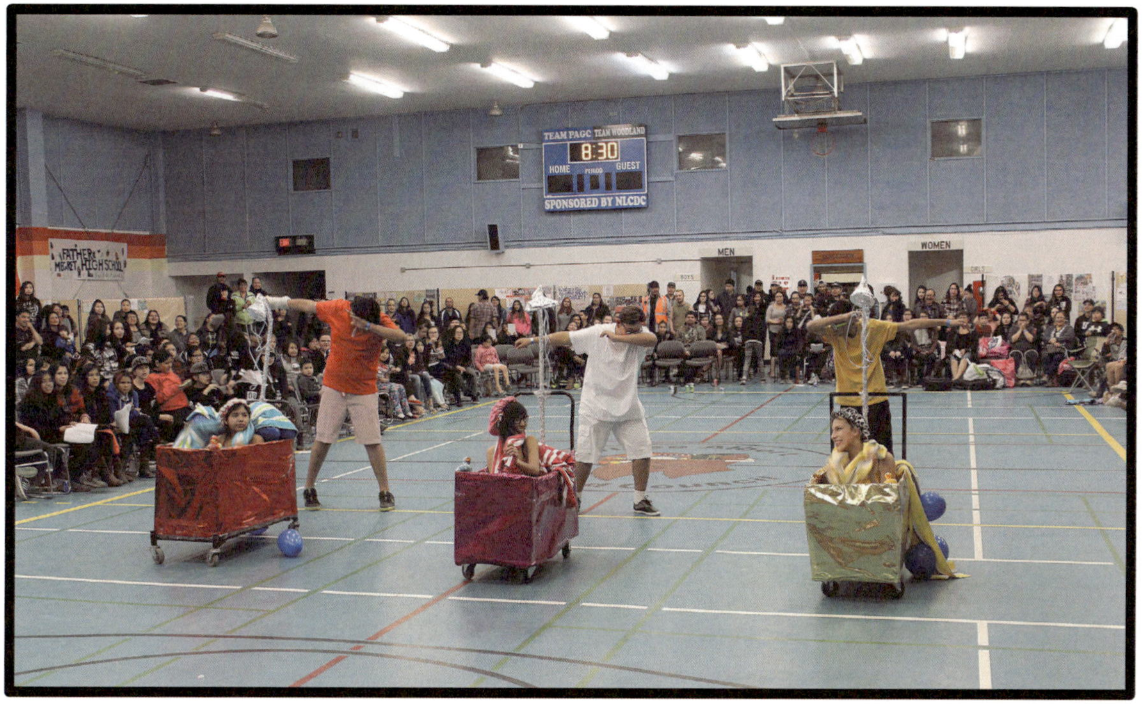
TEAM PAGC TEAM WOODLAND
8:30
HOME
GUEST
SPONSORED BY NLCDC
MEN
WOMEN

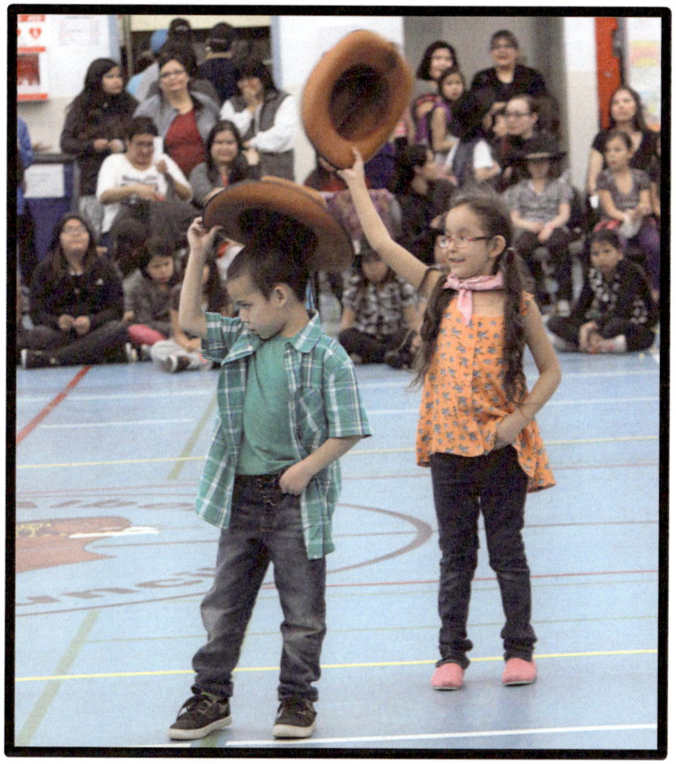

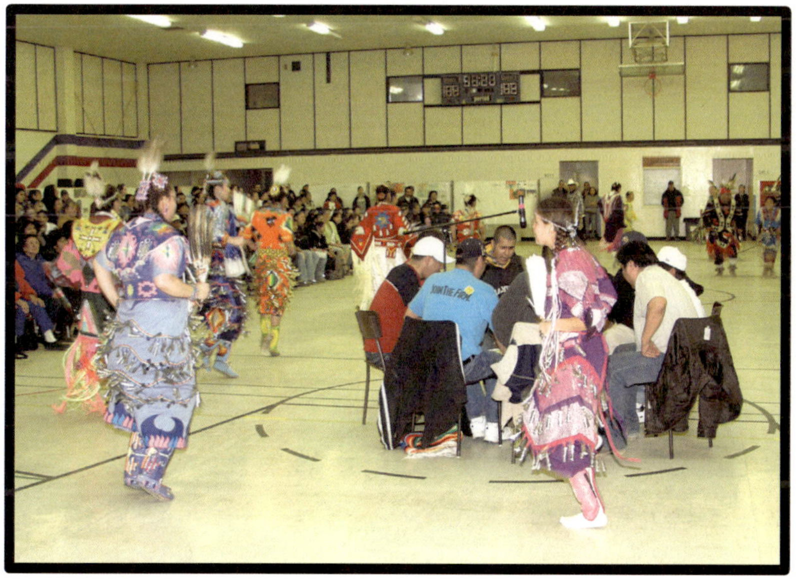

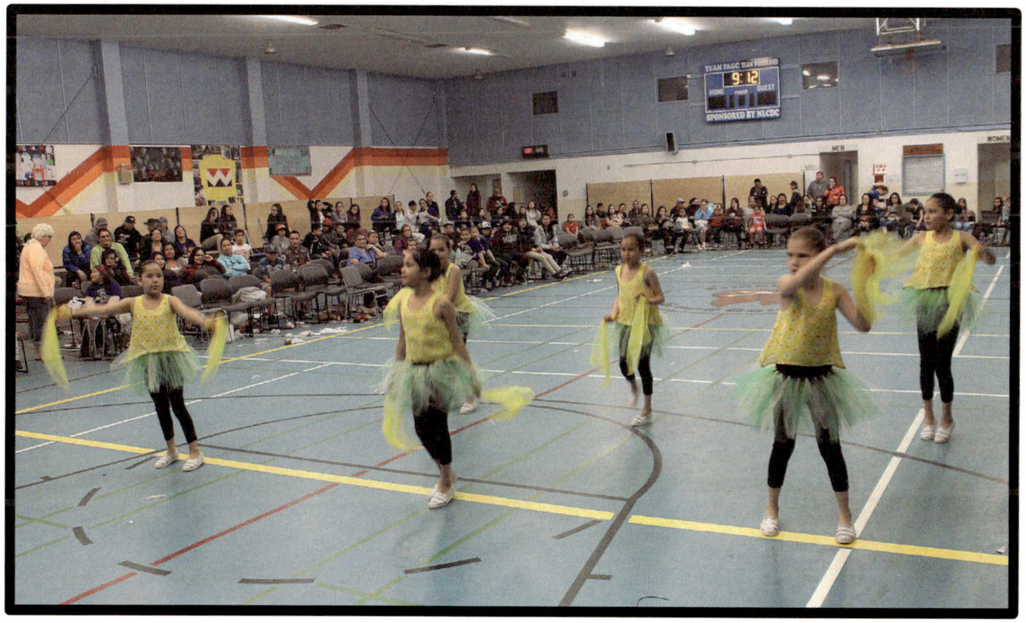
SPONSORED BY NLCDC

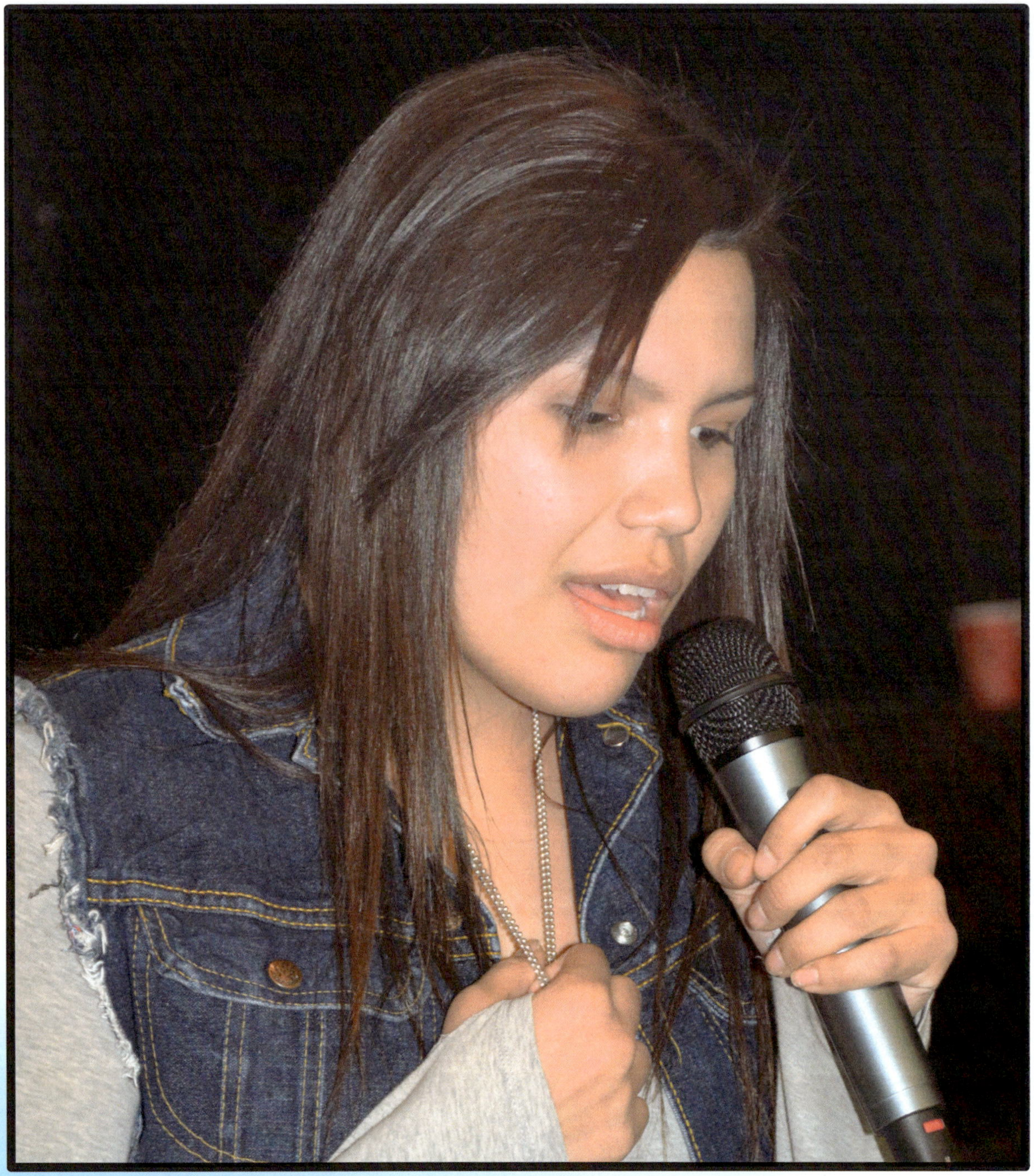

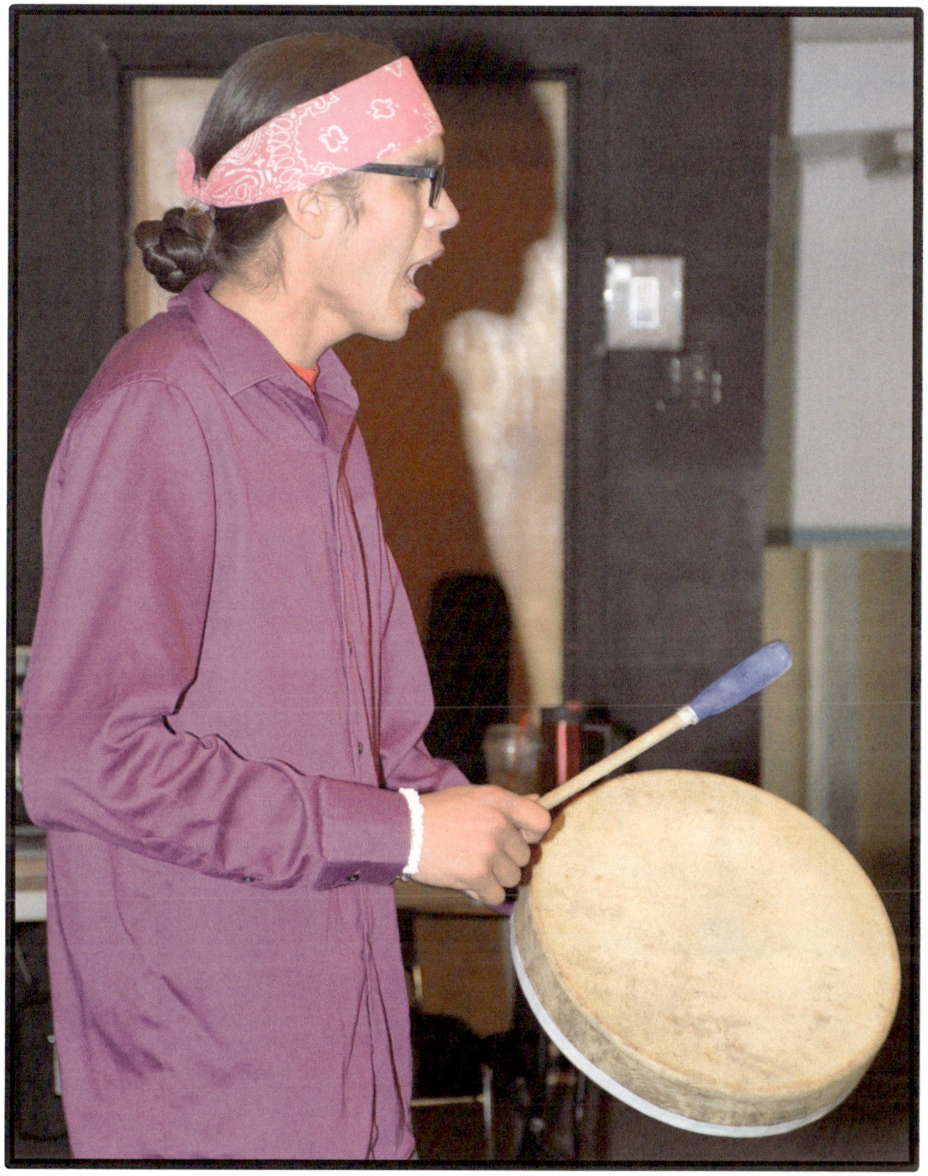

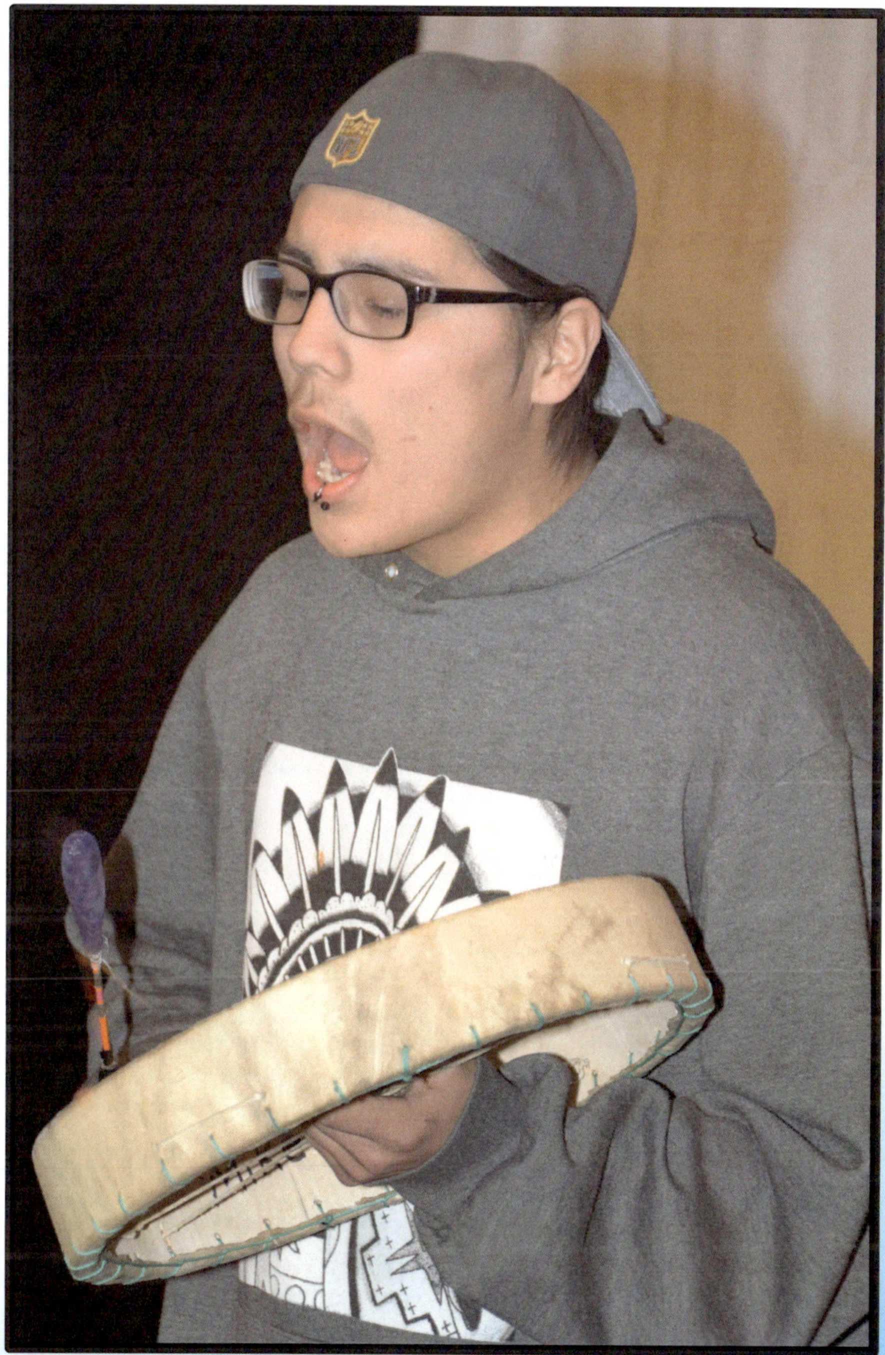

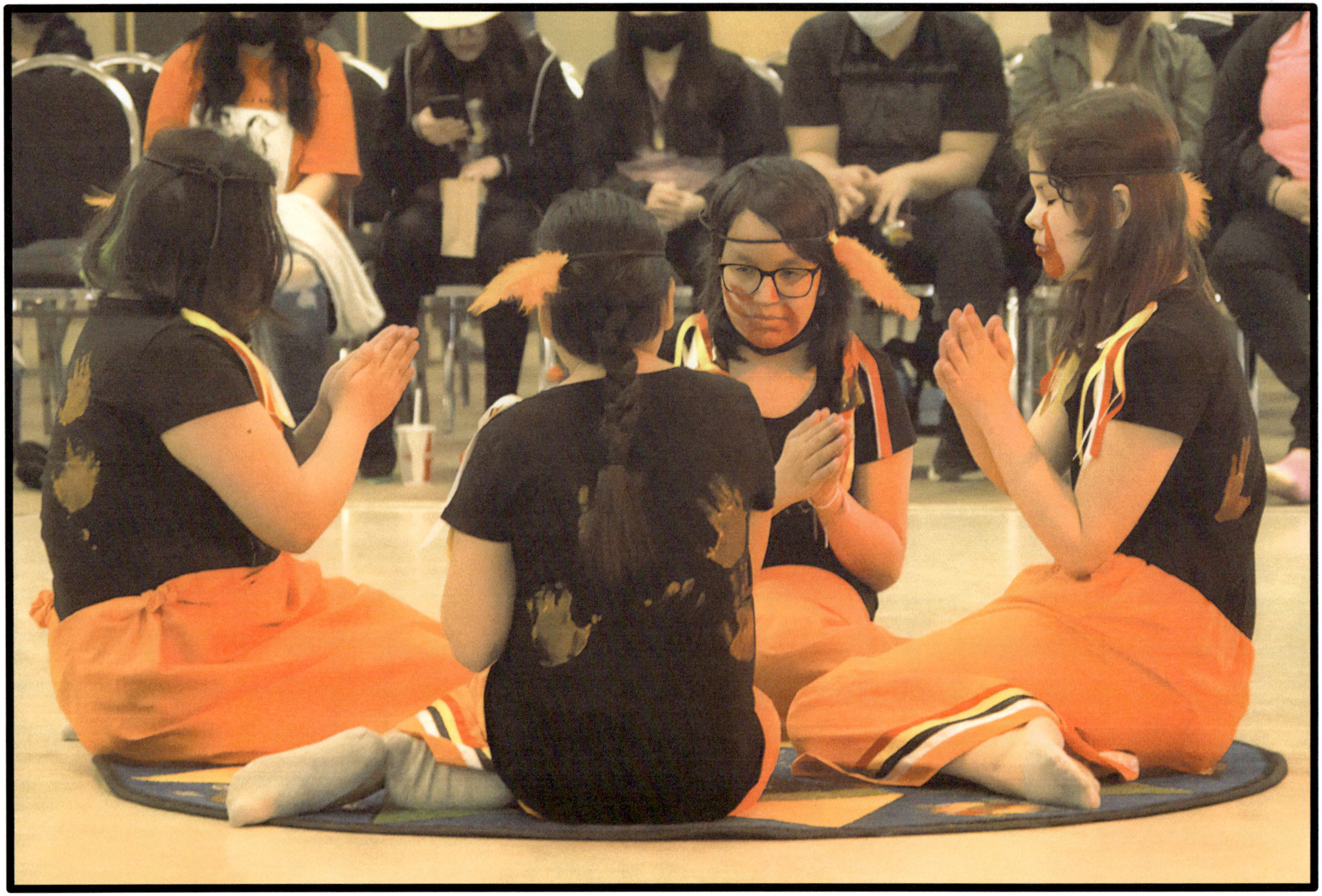

Kiskinwahamawākanak kimosom pwatinahk kihci-kiskinwahamātowikamikos “kimoosom pwatinak” sōhkēciwan-sīpiy ohci ōki. Māmawi-nīmihitowin wīstawāw ka-itēyihtakik ōtē kistapinānihk kihci-wiyasiwēwak ka-pimipayihtācik mētawēstamākēwitohtēwinihk.

Students from Kimosom Pwatinahk Collegiate in Deschambeault Lake, SK perform during the group creative dance competition at the 2022 PAGC Fine Arts Festival.

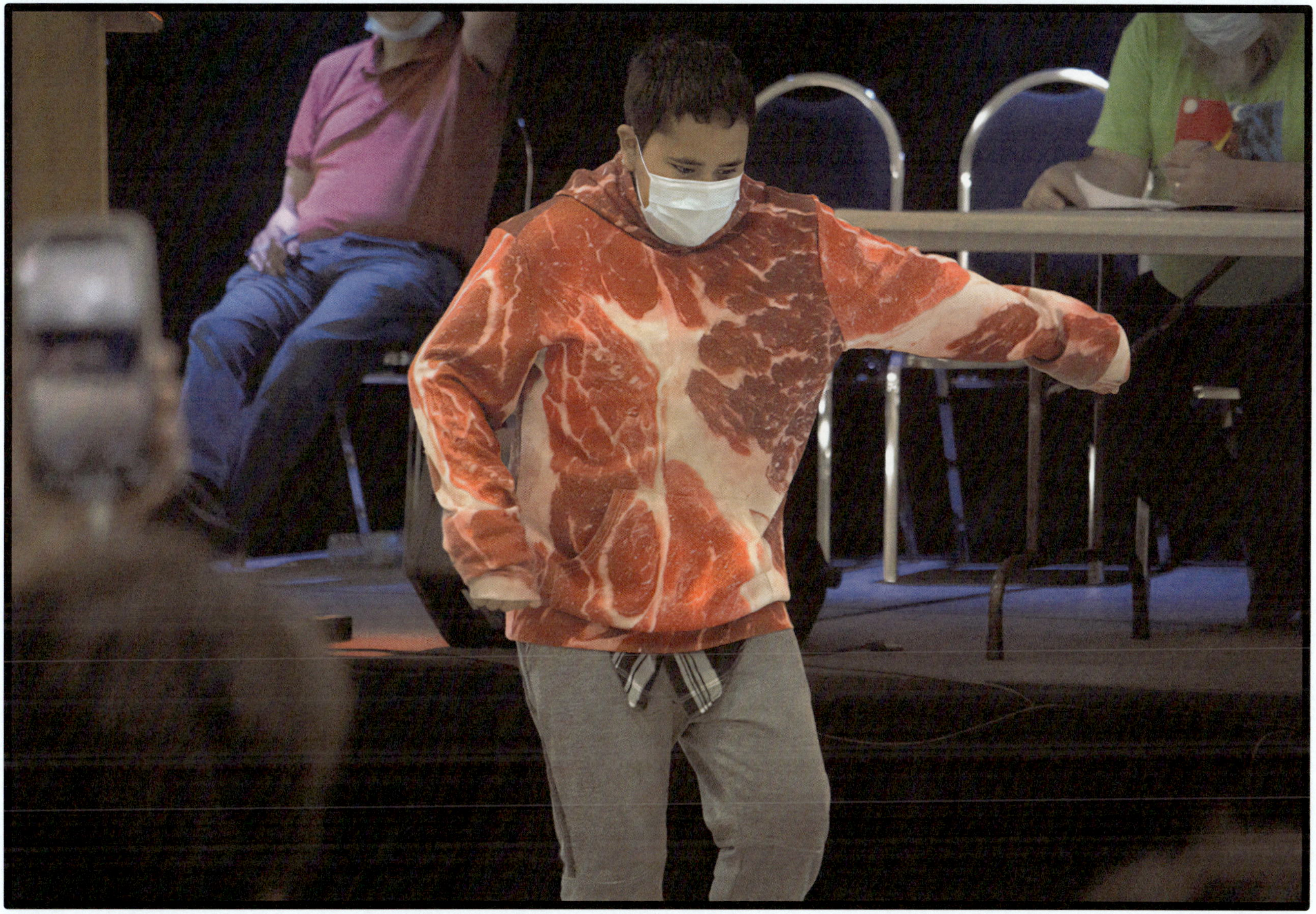

Tēpakohp kapahisotahēt kiniskinwahahamawākan nathan bell owiyasiwēwikimāw myles venne kiskinwahamātowikamik air ronge ohci. Pēh-pēyak ka-itēyihtakik kā-isi-nīmihitocik ōtē mētawēstamākēw itohtēwinihk nīsitanaw nīsosāp āskiy kakī-ispayik.

Grade 7 student, Nathan Bell, from Senator Myles Venne School in Air Ronge, performs during the individual creative dance competition at the 2022 PAGC Fine Arts Festival.

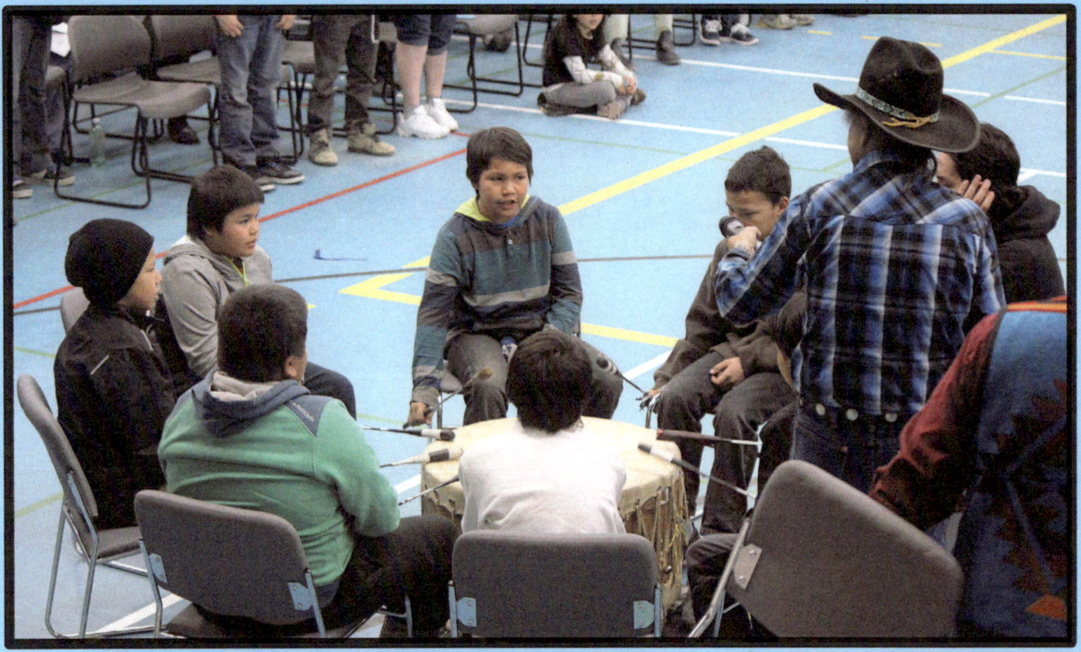

Kiskinwahamawākanak kī-mātwēhikēwak ēkotēhk kistapinānihk kihci-wiyasiwēwak ka-pimipayihtacik mētawestamākēw-itōhtēwinihk

Left: Students drumming at PAGC Fine Arts Festival.

Kiskinwahamawākanak ayamihēwiyiniw gamache kiskisototawāw kiskinwahamātowikamik ohci ōki. Clayton adam jr., latisha olson, amelia toutsaint, dominik whitedeer, zanniah toutsaint, abigail isadore ēkwa miley fern.

Below: Students from Father Gamache Memorial School (from left to right): Clayton Adam Jr., Latisha Olson, Amelia Toutsaint, Dominik Whitedeer, Zanniah Toutsaint, Abigail Isadore & Miley Fern

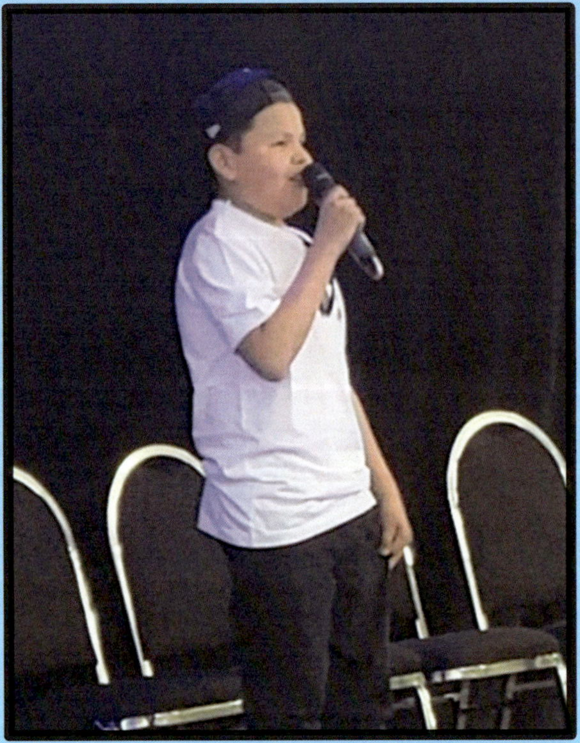

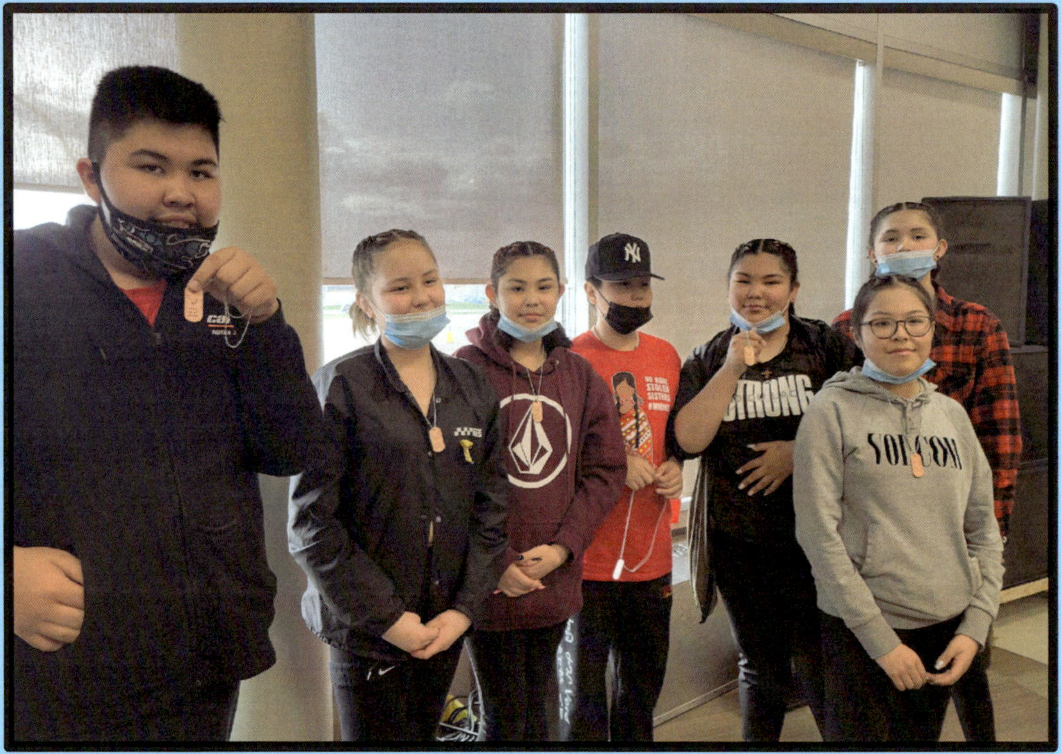

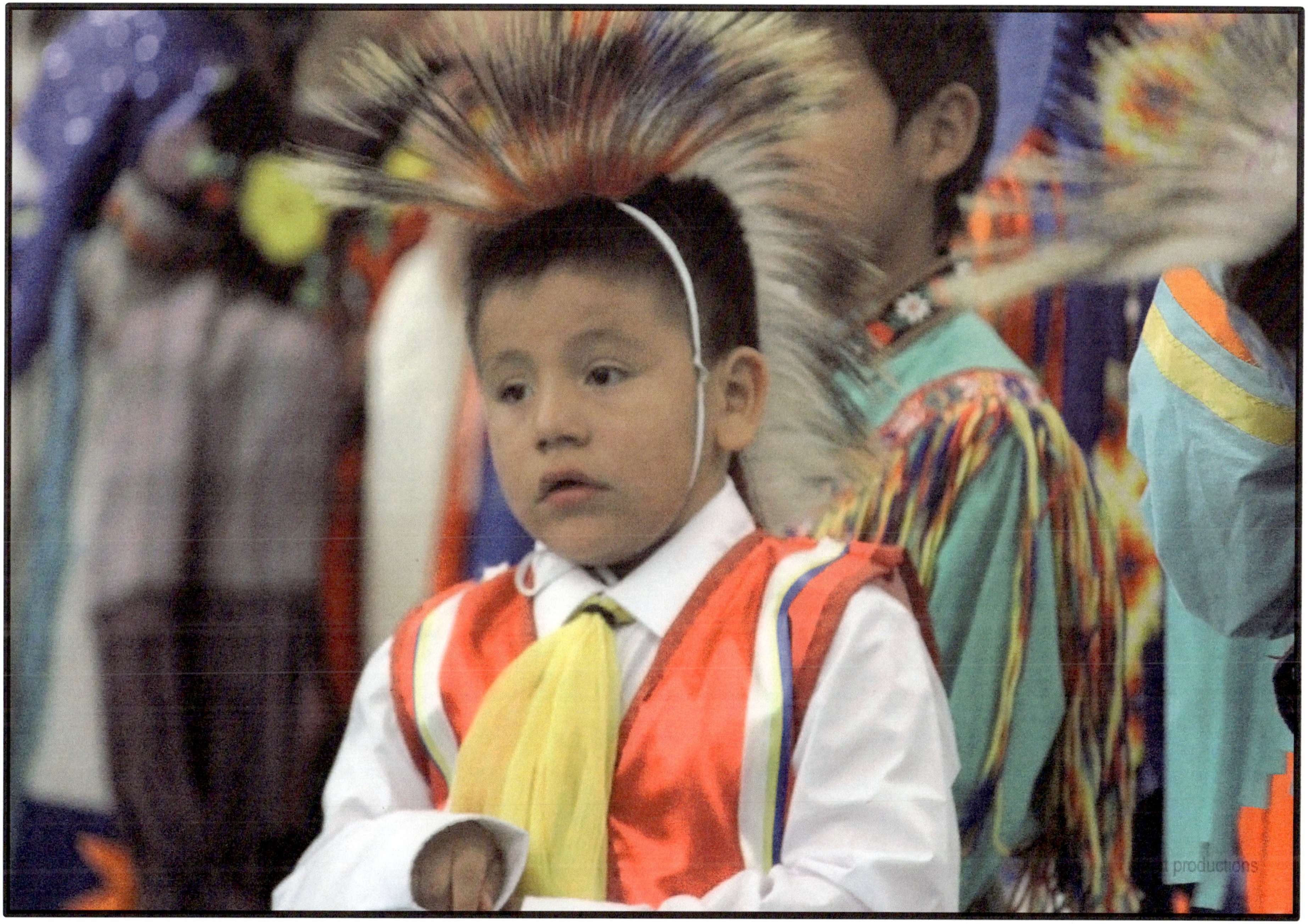

Photo Credit: Marcel Petit at m.pet productions

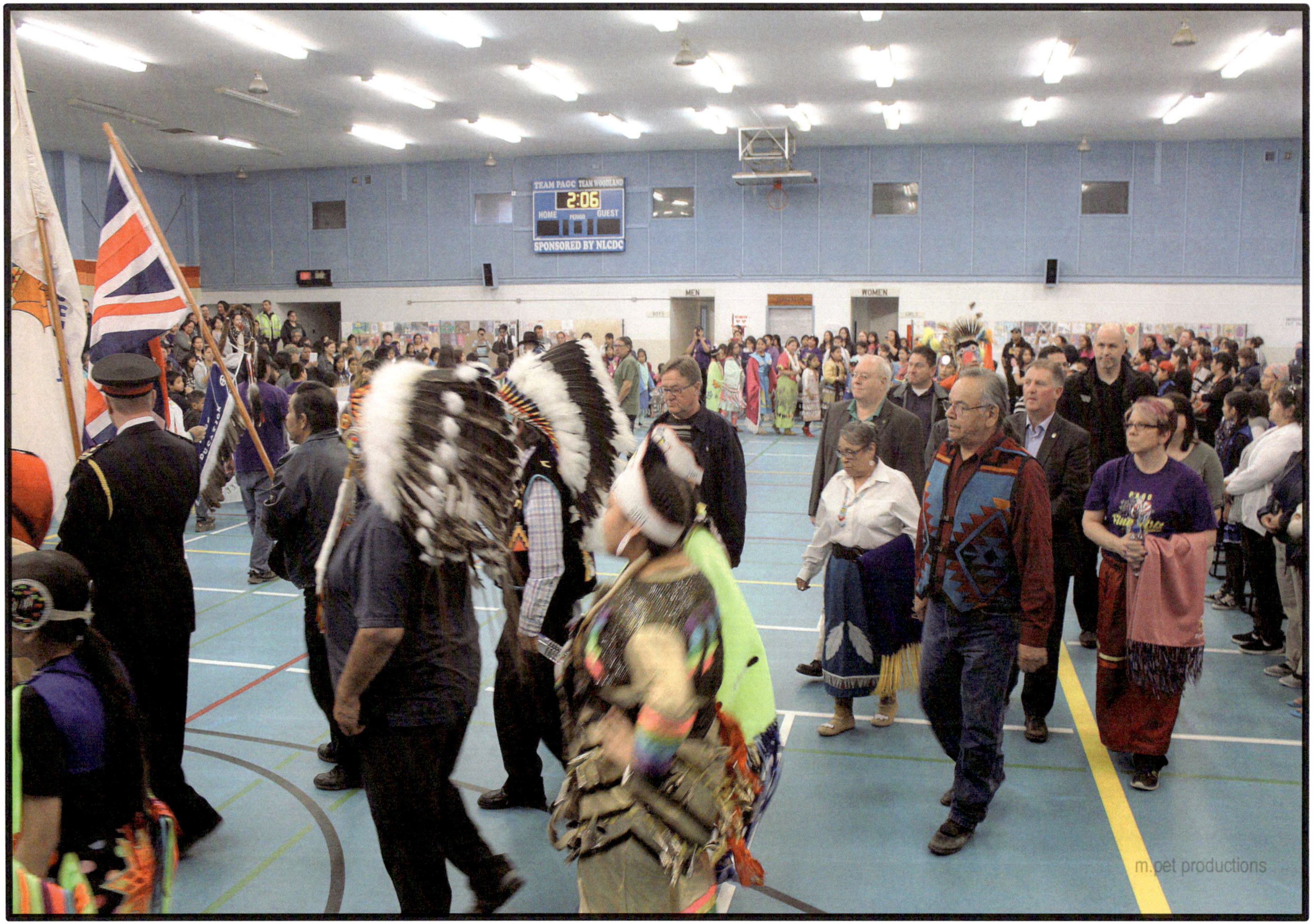

Photo Credit: Marcel Petit at m.pet productions

ARTWORK

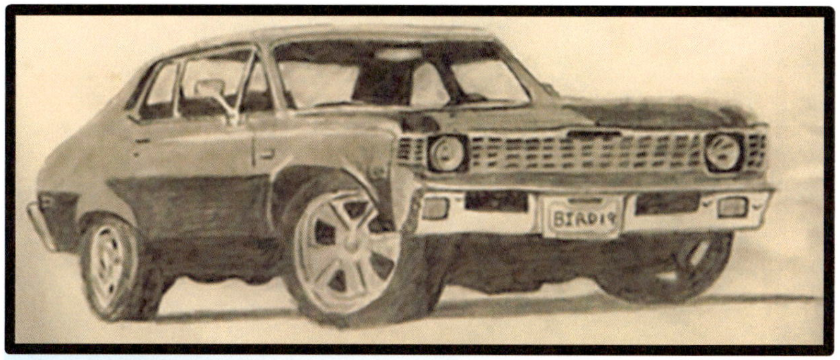

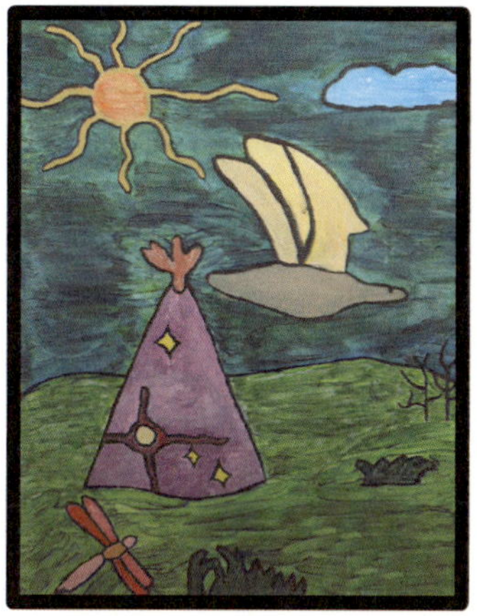

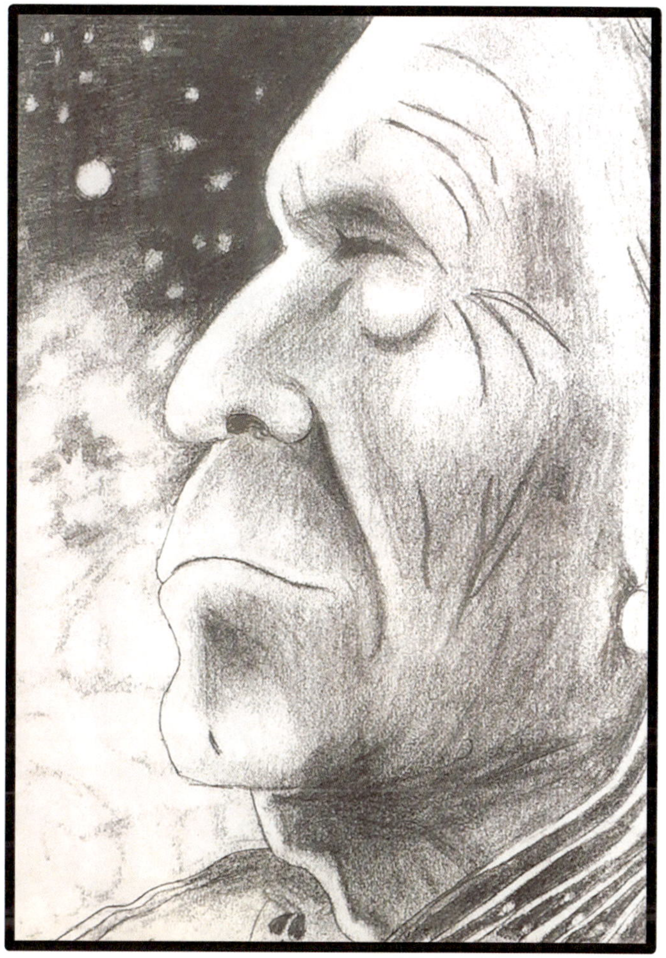

Above: "Respect" - Pencil drawing by Lucas Cook

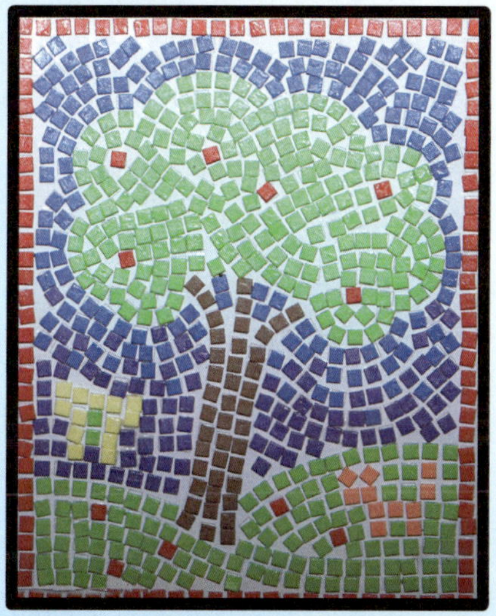

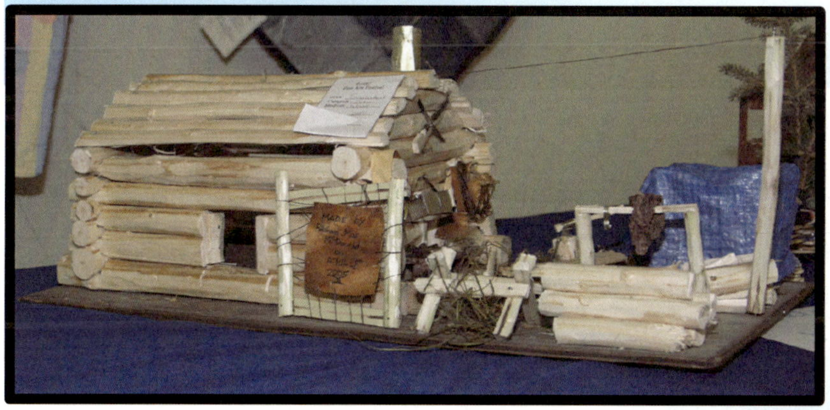

Wood Sculpture by Richard May McDonald

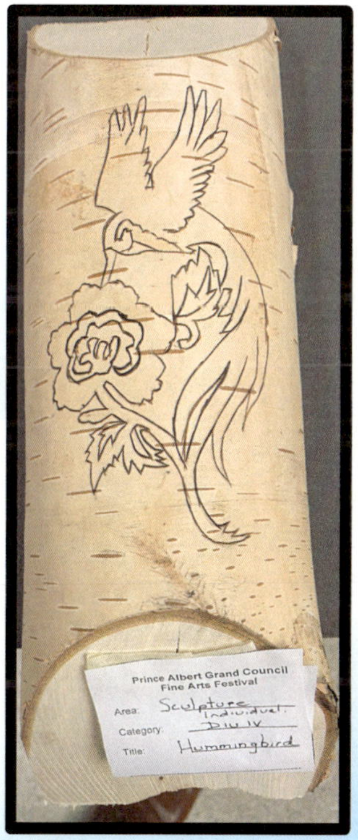

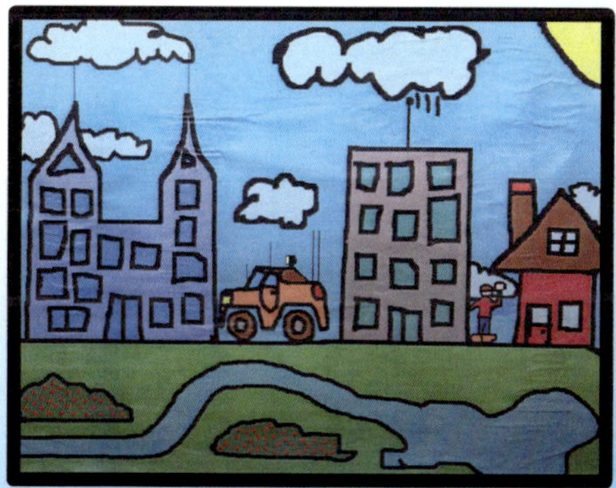

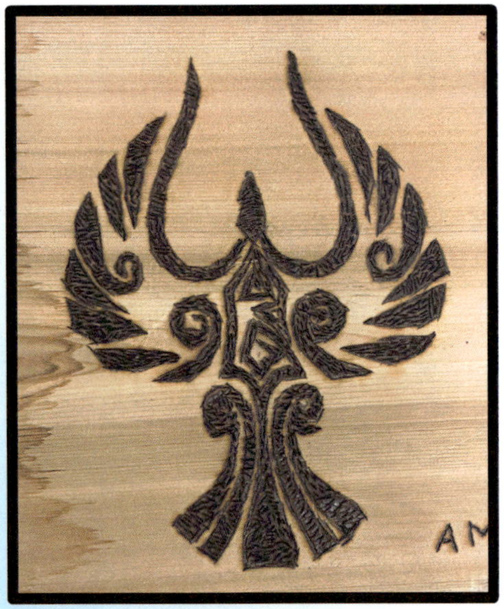

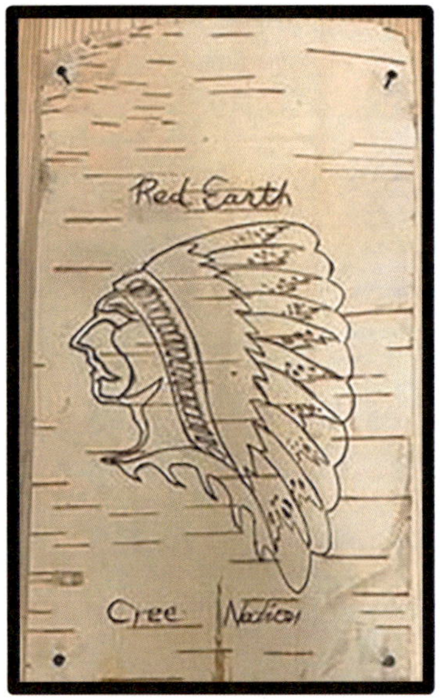

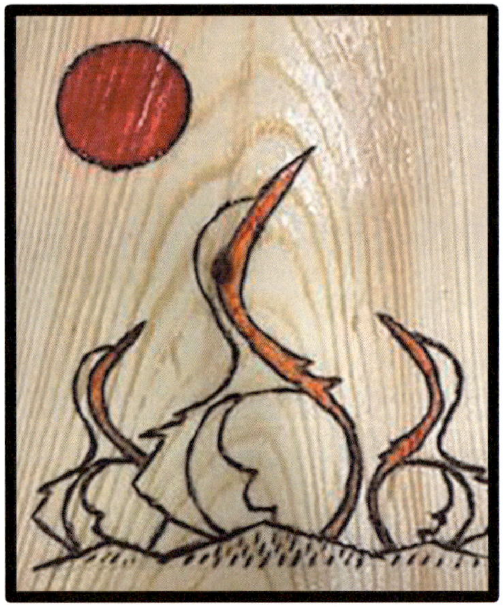

Ēkonik ōki kiskinwahamawākanak ka-mawinēhikēcik awina kakwē-miyo-tāpasinahikēt. Ēkōma pēyak itahkamikisēwin ē-atoskēmakak ōma ka-kakwē-nihtā-nēhiyawē-pīkiskwēcik. Kistapinānihk kihci-wiyasiwēwinahk ka-pimipayihtācik. Ā- thap-āsk-āw, sākāstēnohk, misi-sakāhk, ēkwa sāwanohk askihk ohtohtēwak.

Students from each of the PAGC sectors (Athabasca, Eastern, Woodland and Southern) compete in visual arts. This is one of the platforms that supports the efforts of Indigenous communities to reclaim, revitalize, maintain and strengthen their languages.

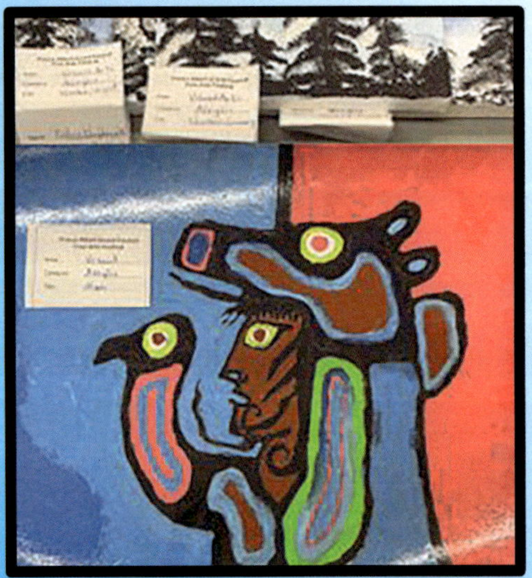

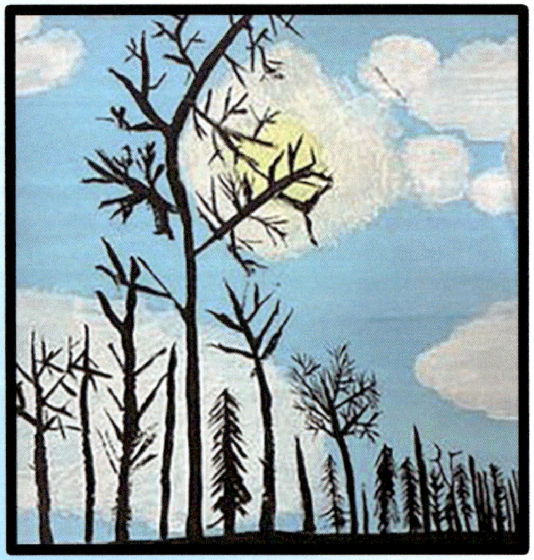

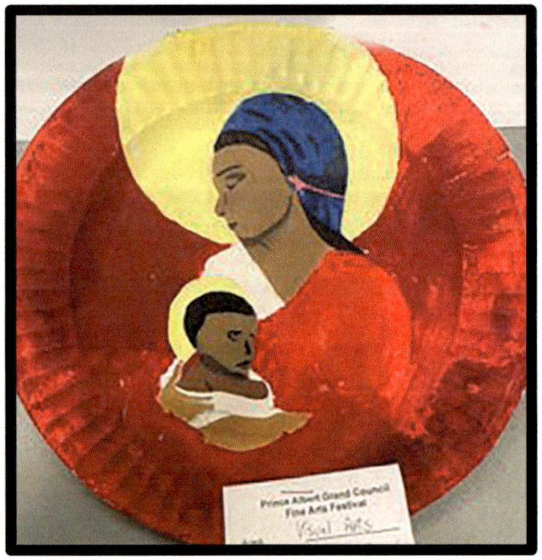

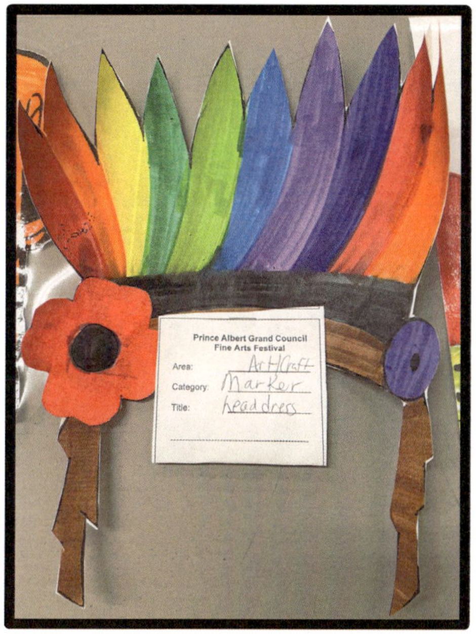

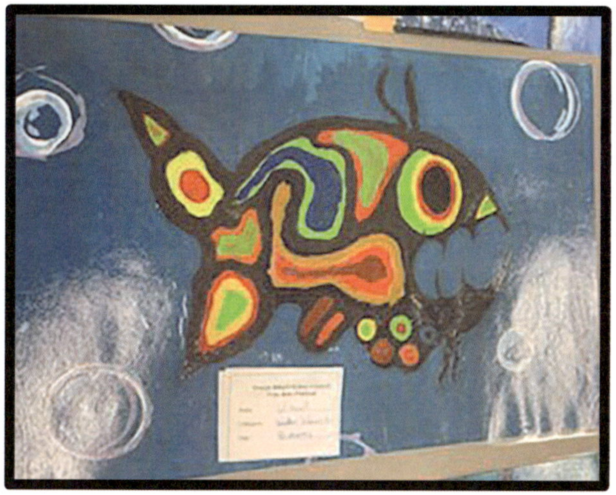

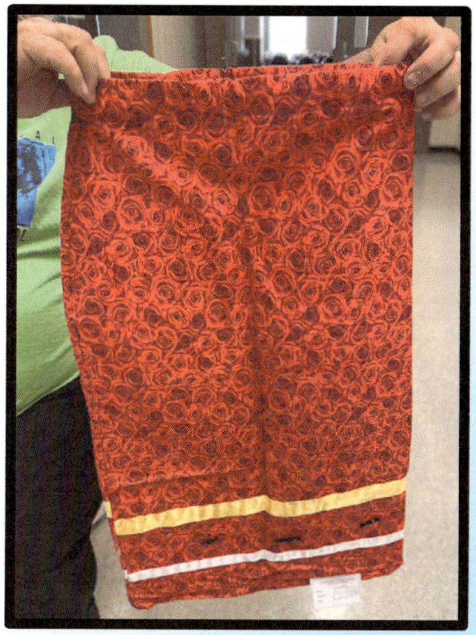

Kotaka pāh-pītos osīhcikēwina tāpiskōc masinipēhikēwina, iyinito-isīhcikēwin, mistikowa-osīhcikēwina ē-wīcihitomakāhk awiyak ka-osīhcikēt.

Other unique projects made by students include paintings, crafts, and wood projects that enrich creativity.

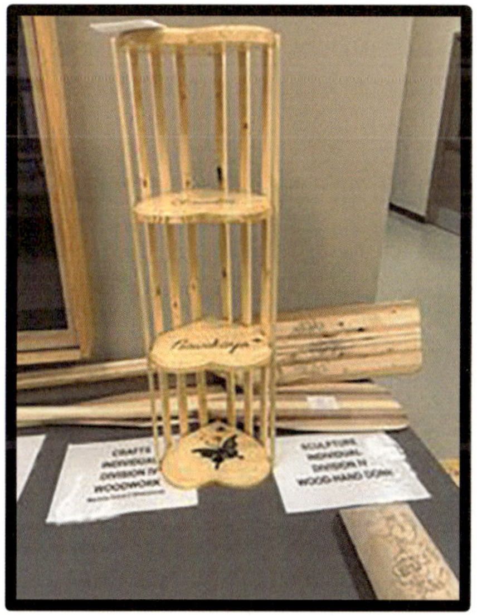

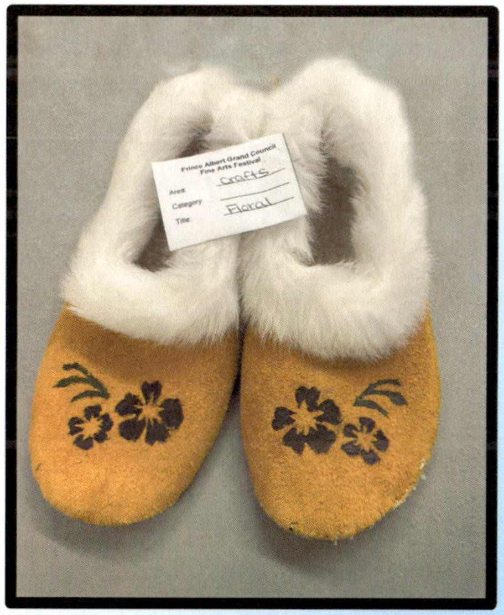

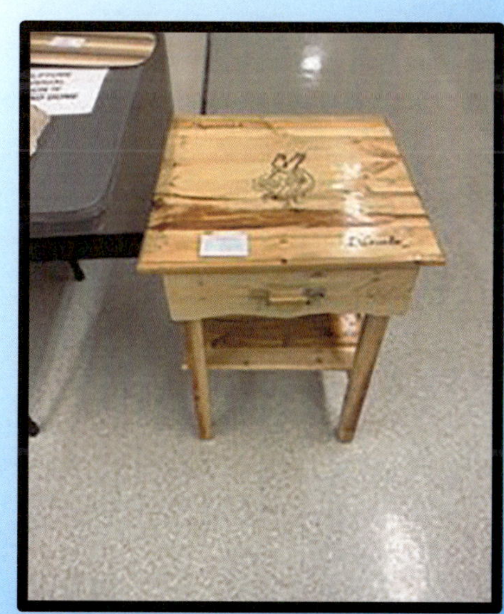

Otaskīwin māmawi-ātahka-mikisēwina āpatēyihtākwāna ēko-ta ka-māmawipayicik. Ēmēkosicik nisitohtamowin ēkwa nakacihtāwin ōma iyinito-ayisiyiniwiwin.

Land-based activities are integrated into the Fine Arts Festival, which give students an opportunity to demonstrate their understanding and skills specific to Indigenous Knowledge.

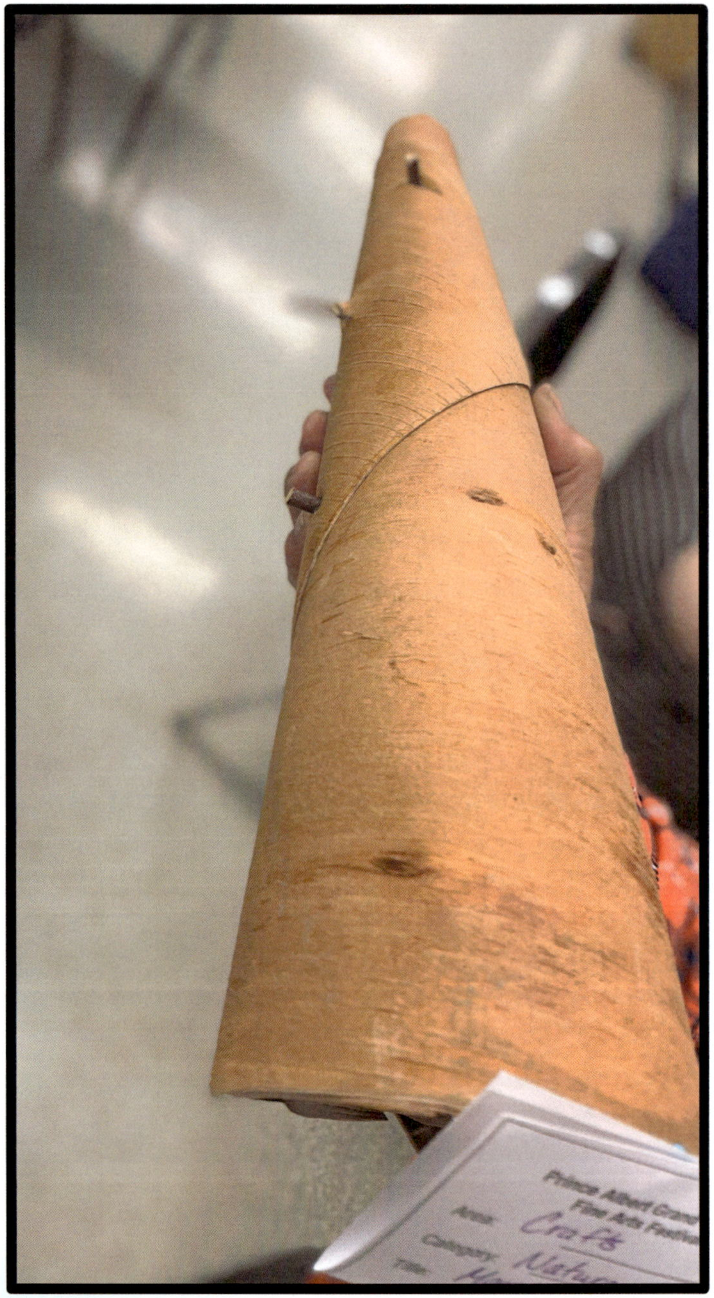

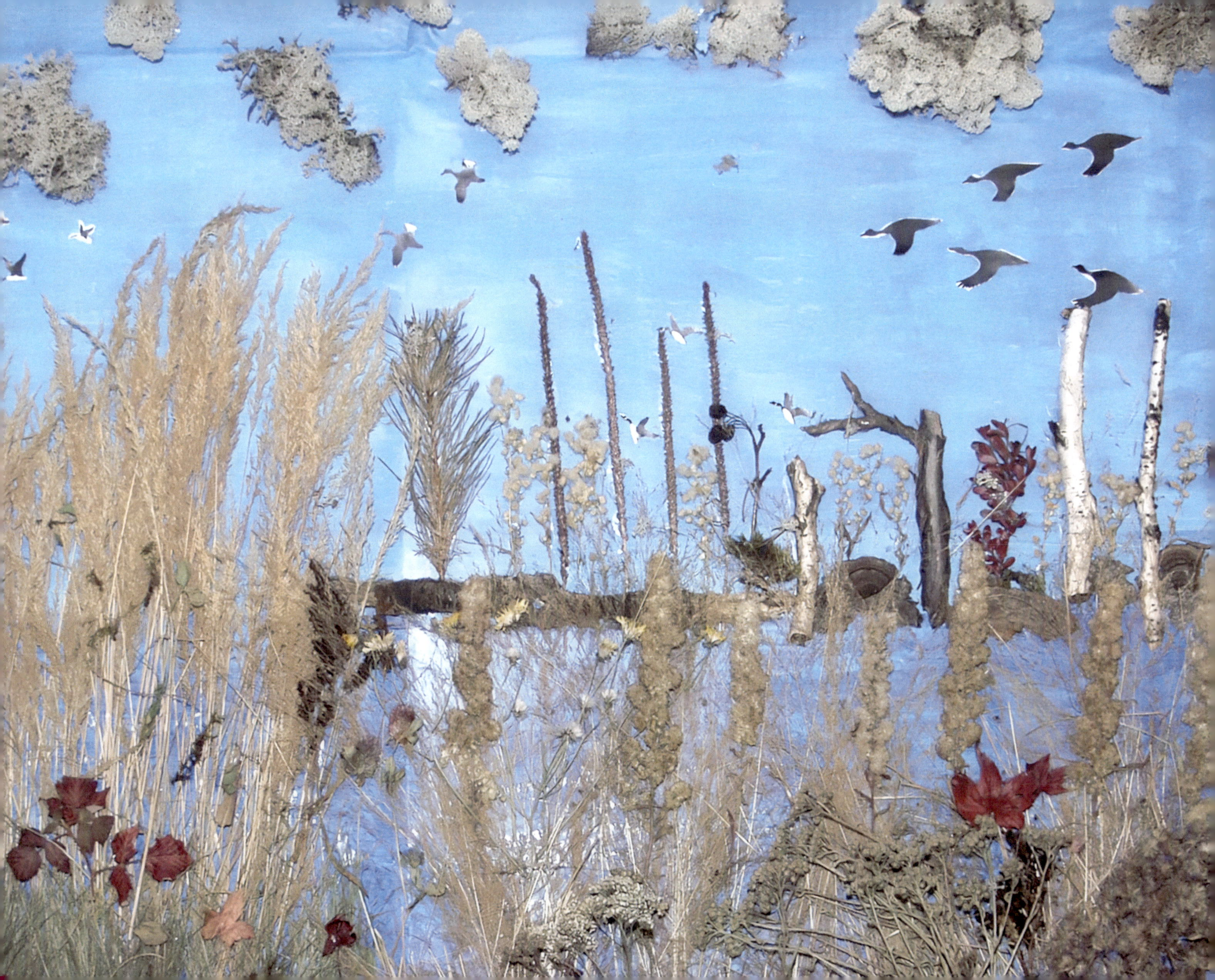

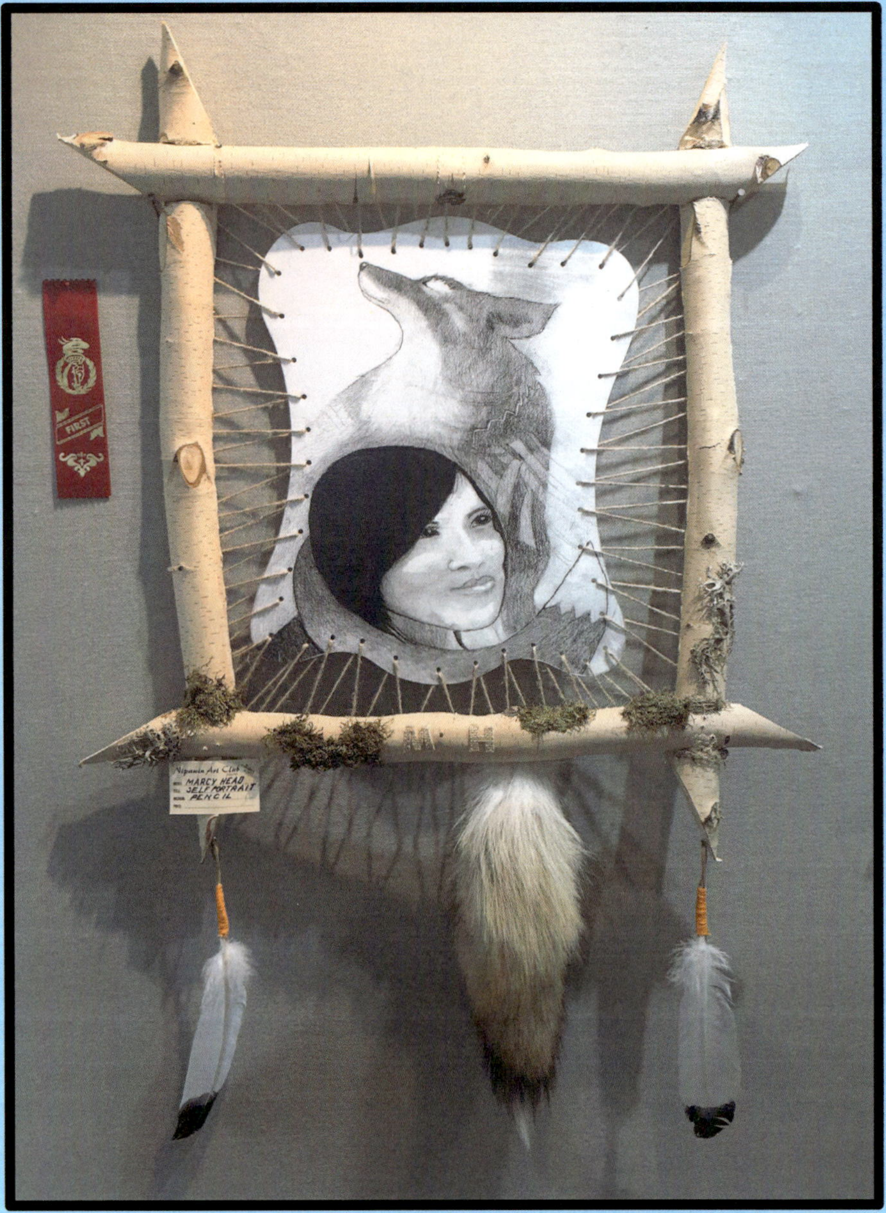

Ēmasināsot awa marcy head. Ētāpasinahikāsot.

Self-portrait: Pencil Drawing by Marcy Head

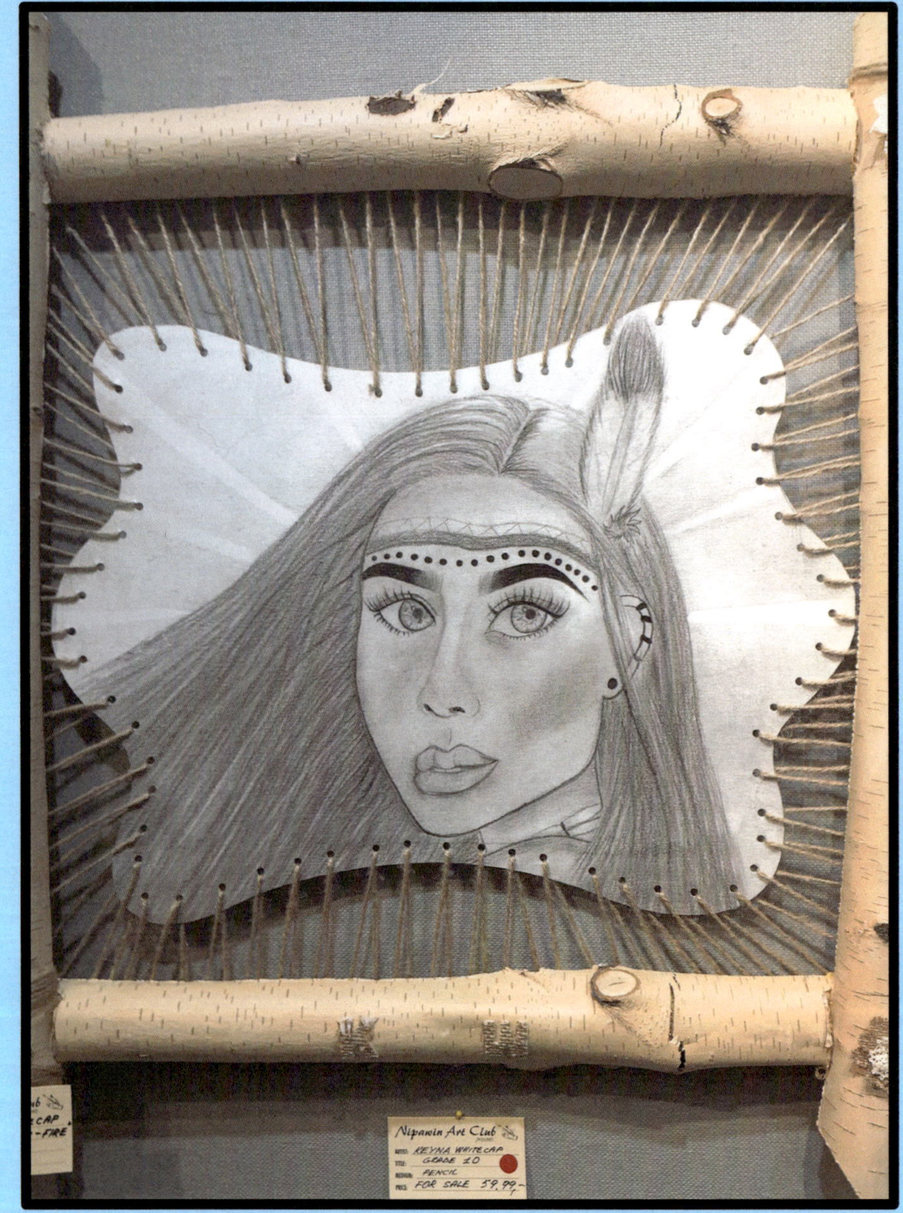

Ē-tāpasinahwāt "ugne-fire-iskotēw".

"Ugne-Fire-Iskotew": Pencil drawing by Keyna Whitecap

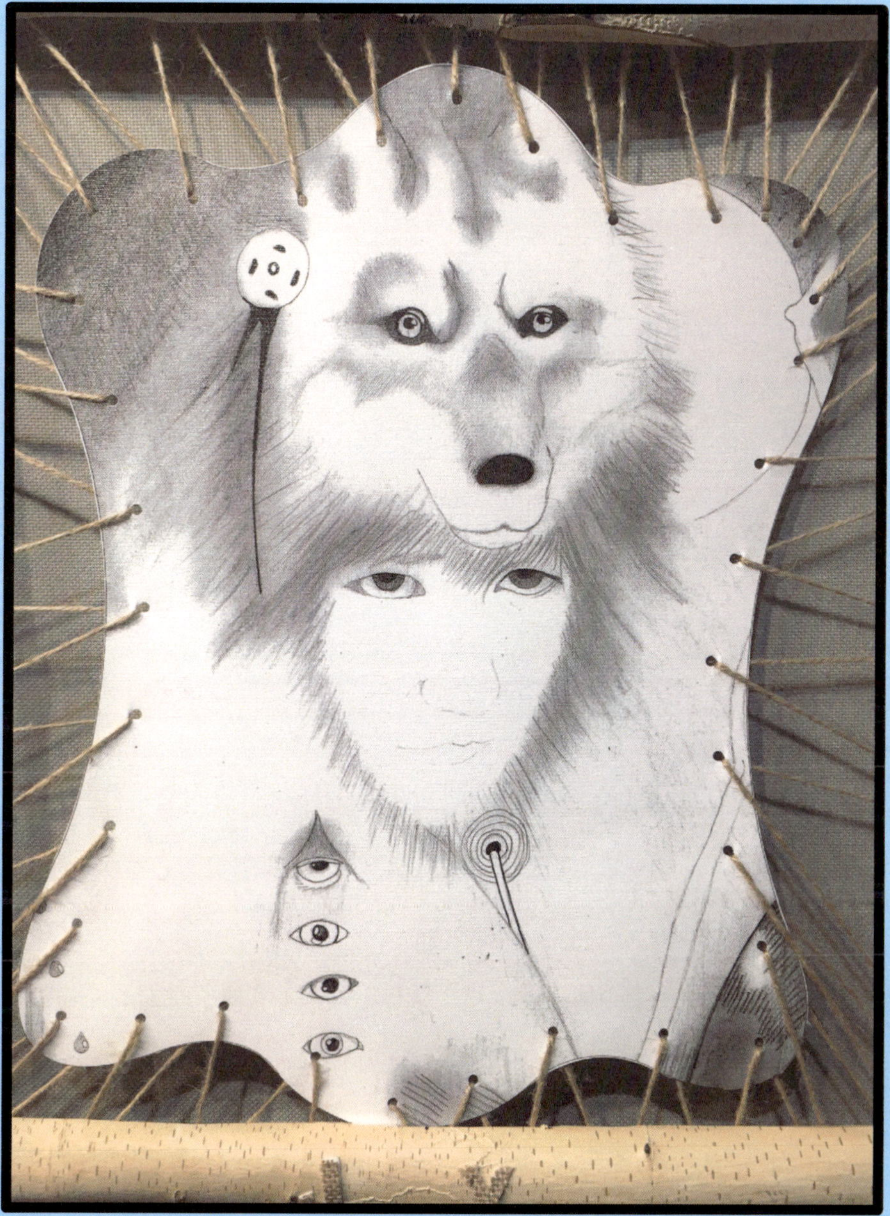

Ē-tāpasināsot jarret young.

Self-portrait: Pencil drawing by Jarret Young

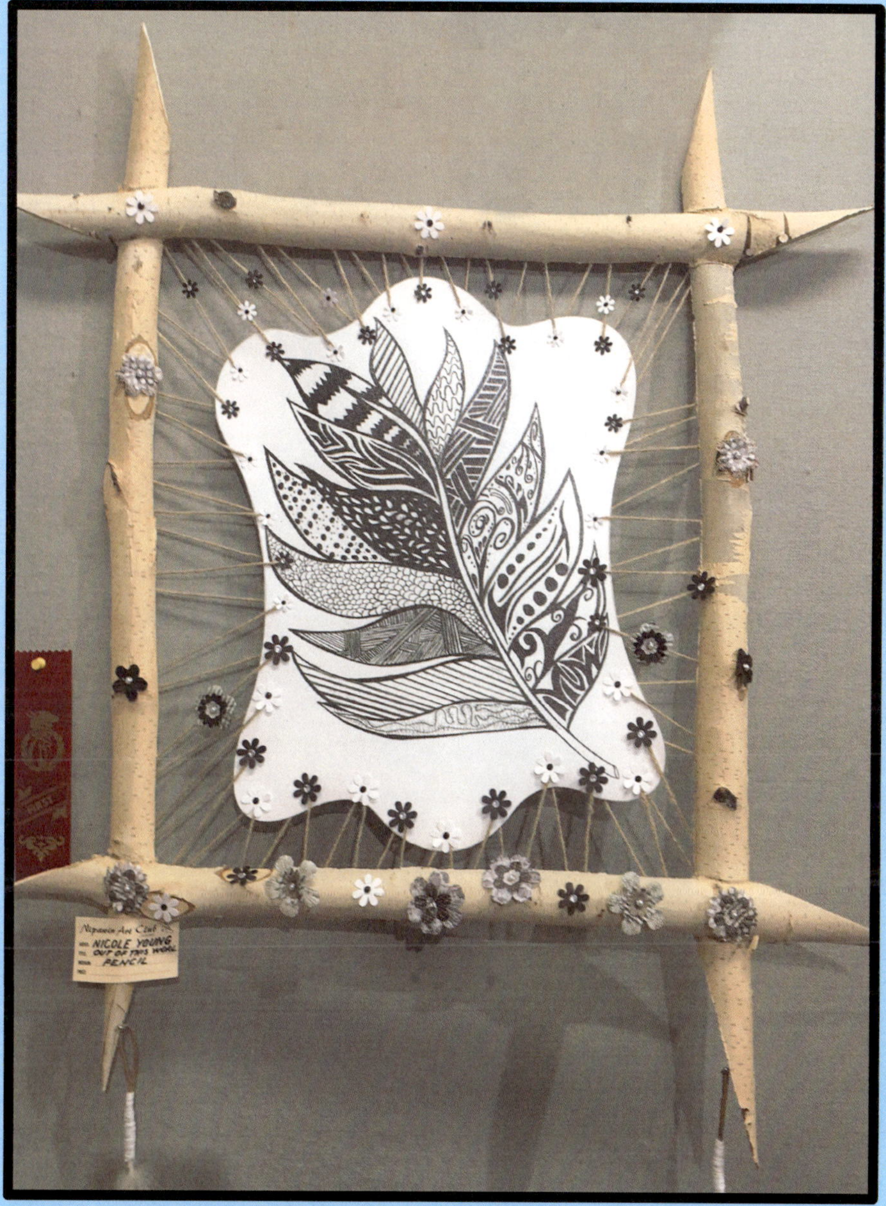

Nicole young otāpasinaham "ohpimē askihk".

"Out of this World": Pencil drawing by Nicole Young

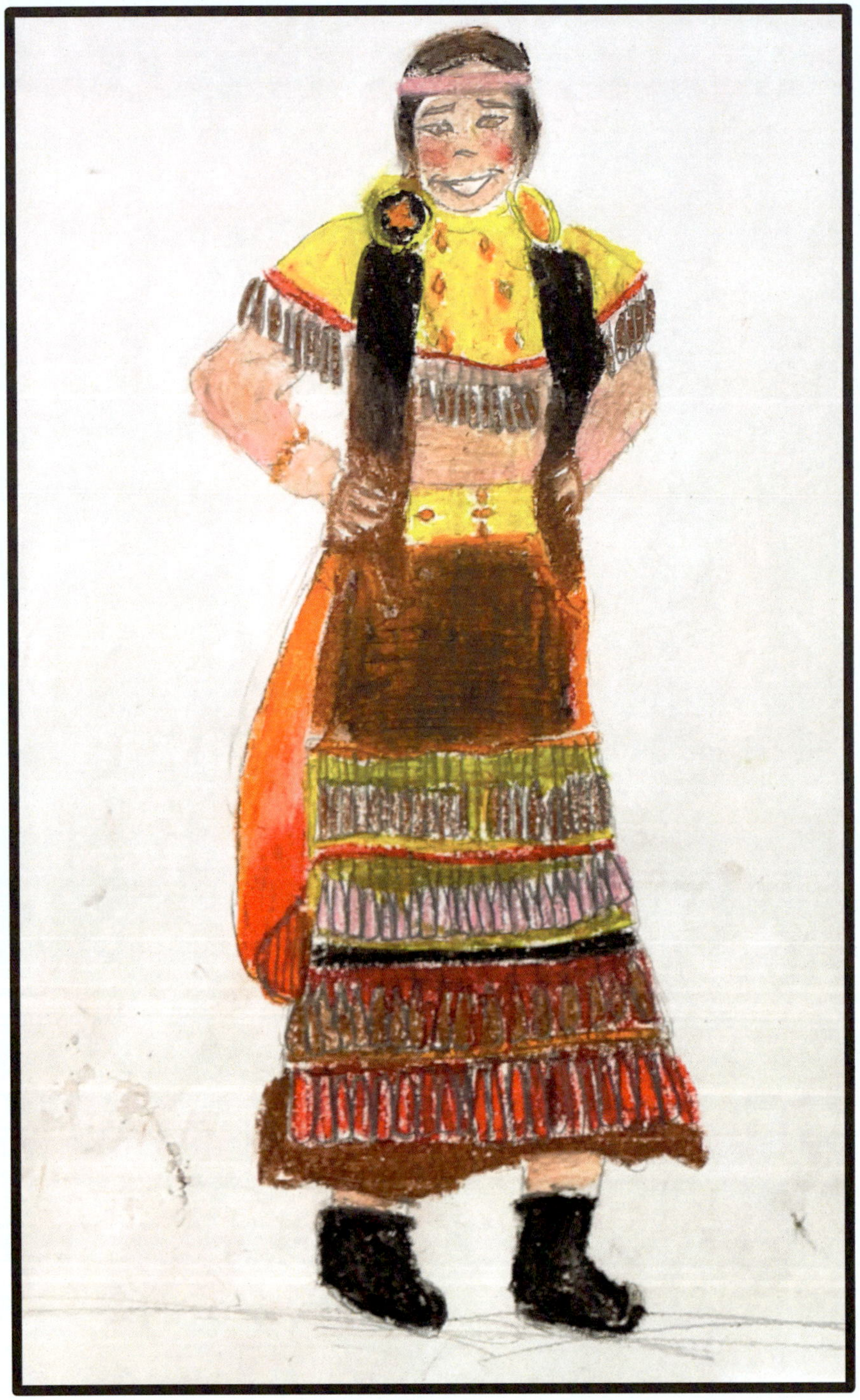

Masināstēwikan ōma ē-isiyihkātēhk “sēwēpayi-pwātisimo-iskwēw”.
Pastel drawing titled “Jingle Dancer”

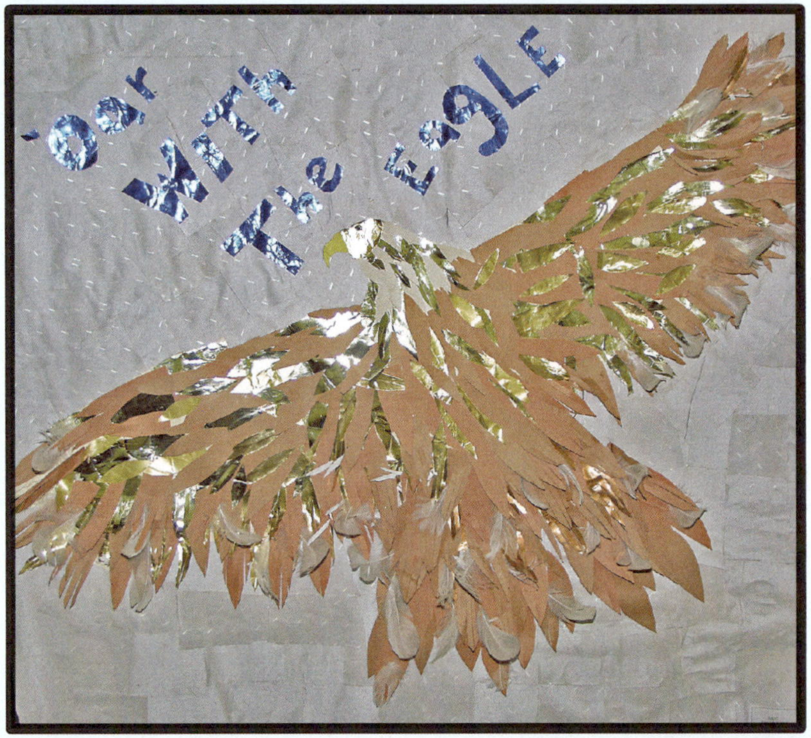

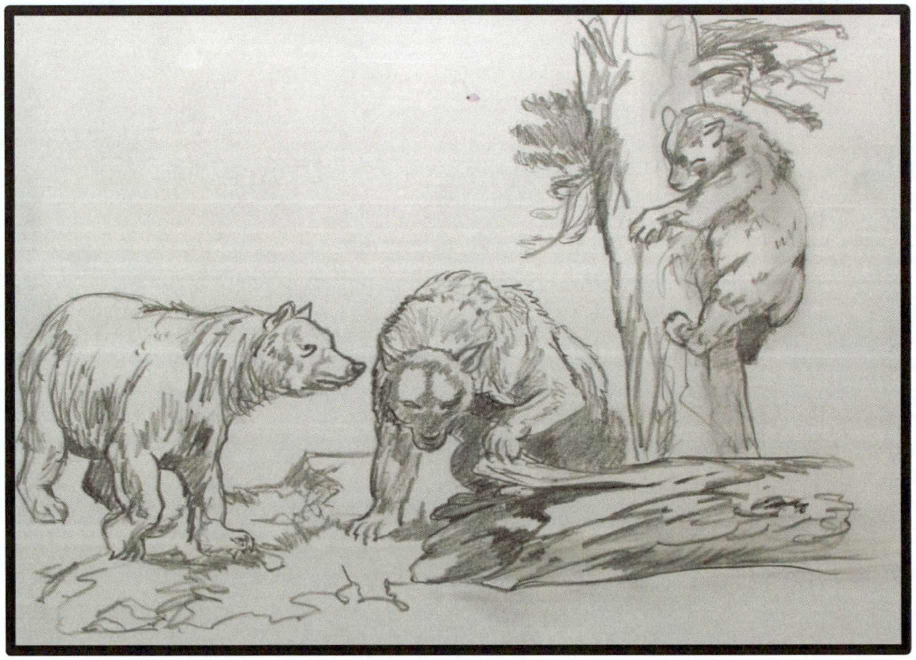

Naspasinahikēwin “maskwak” ē-isiyihkātēhk.
Pencil drawing titled “Bears”

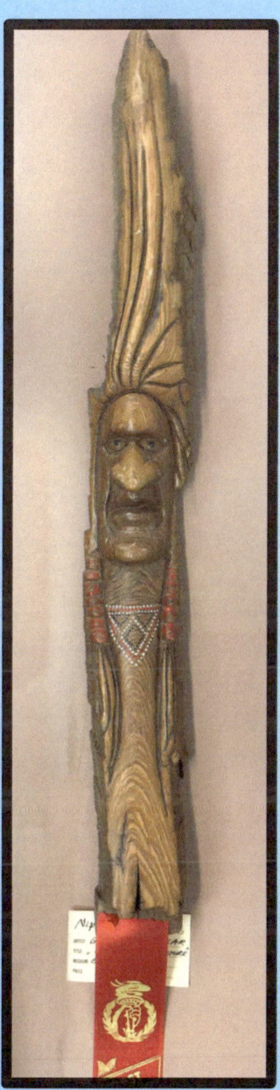

Oyihkocikēwin awa germaine bear ē-osihtāt/ Carving by Germaine Bear

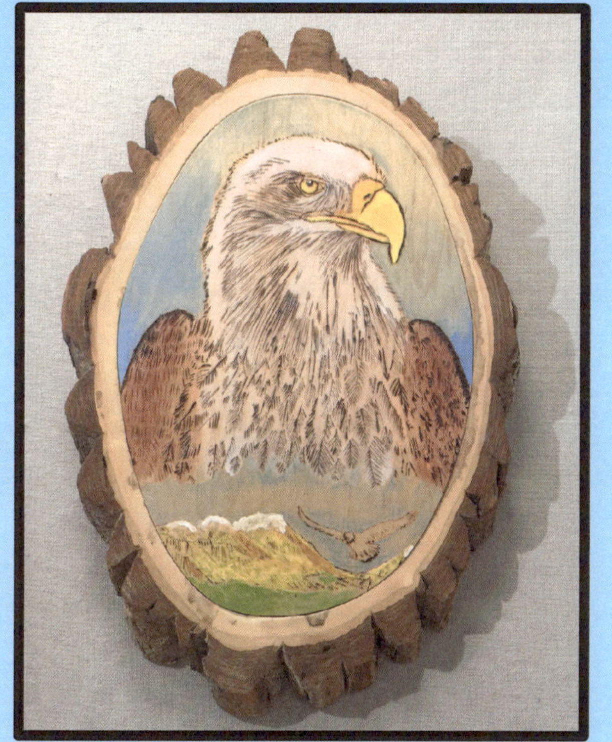

Above: Pyrography by Aiden Lathlin/Iskotēwi-itasinahikēwin aiden lathlin osīhcikēwin
Below: Pencil drawing titled "Christmas Fun"

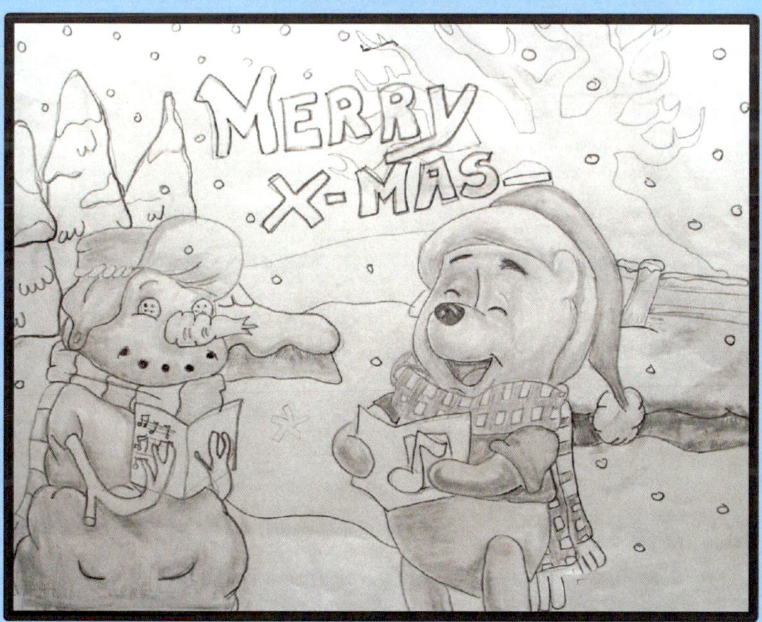

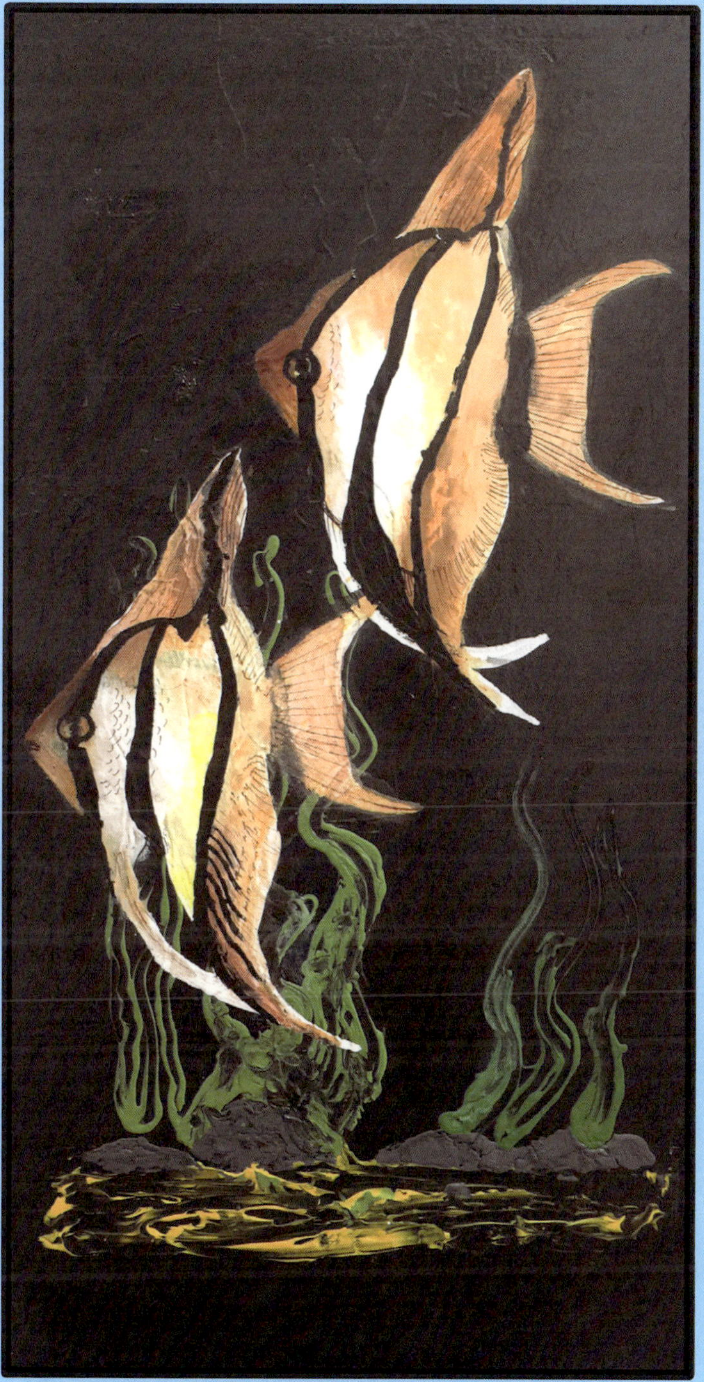

"kinosēwikamik" fawn bear tāpasinaham
"Fish Tank" by Fawn Bear

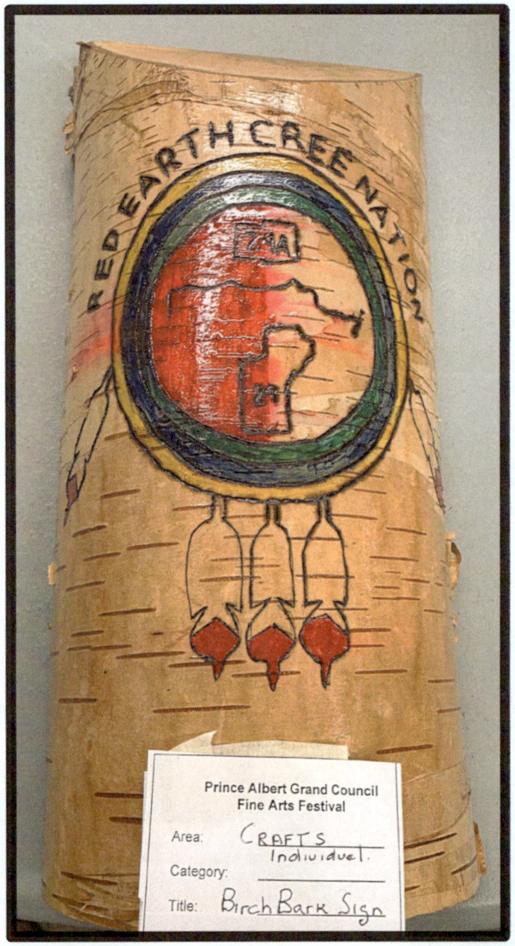

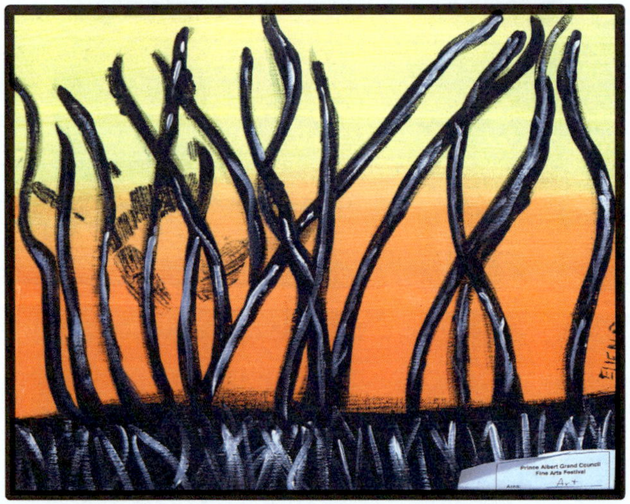

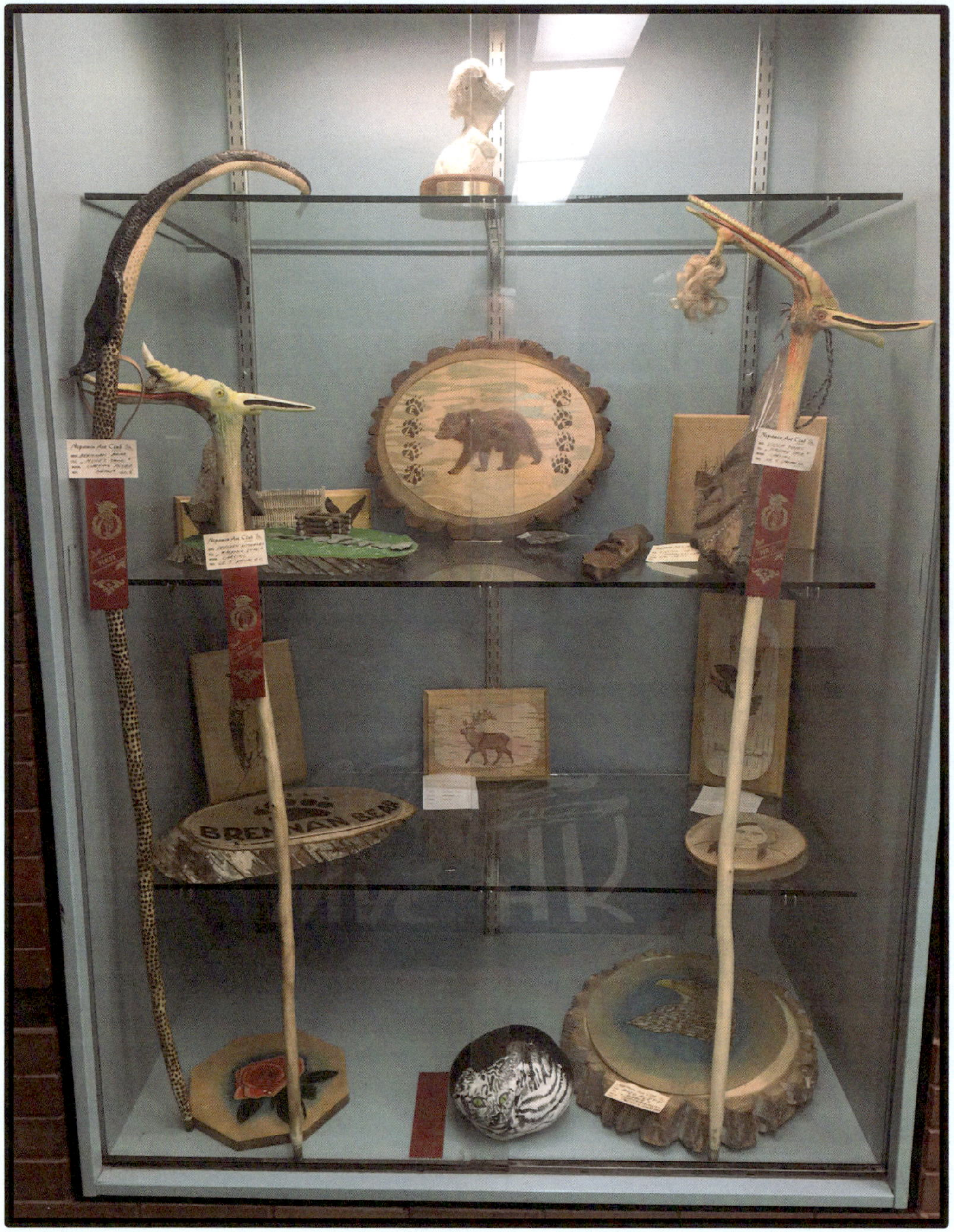

Nistam cahkasinahikana itāpahtihēwina pāhkwāw-sākahikanihk kiskinwahamātowikamik ohci/
First Art Display at Shoal Lake School

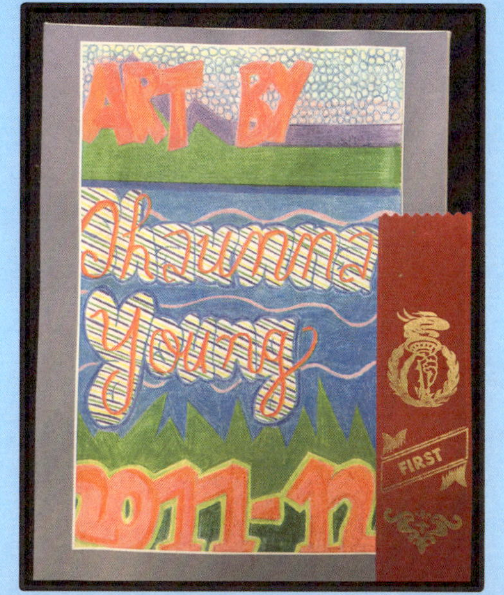
ART BY
Shaunna
Young
2011-12
FIRST

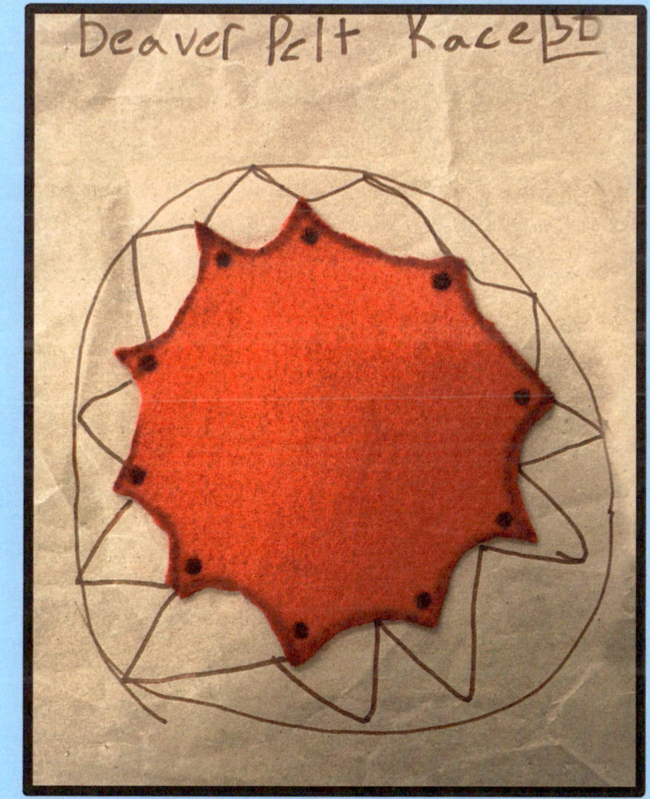
Beaver Pelt Race

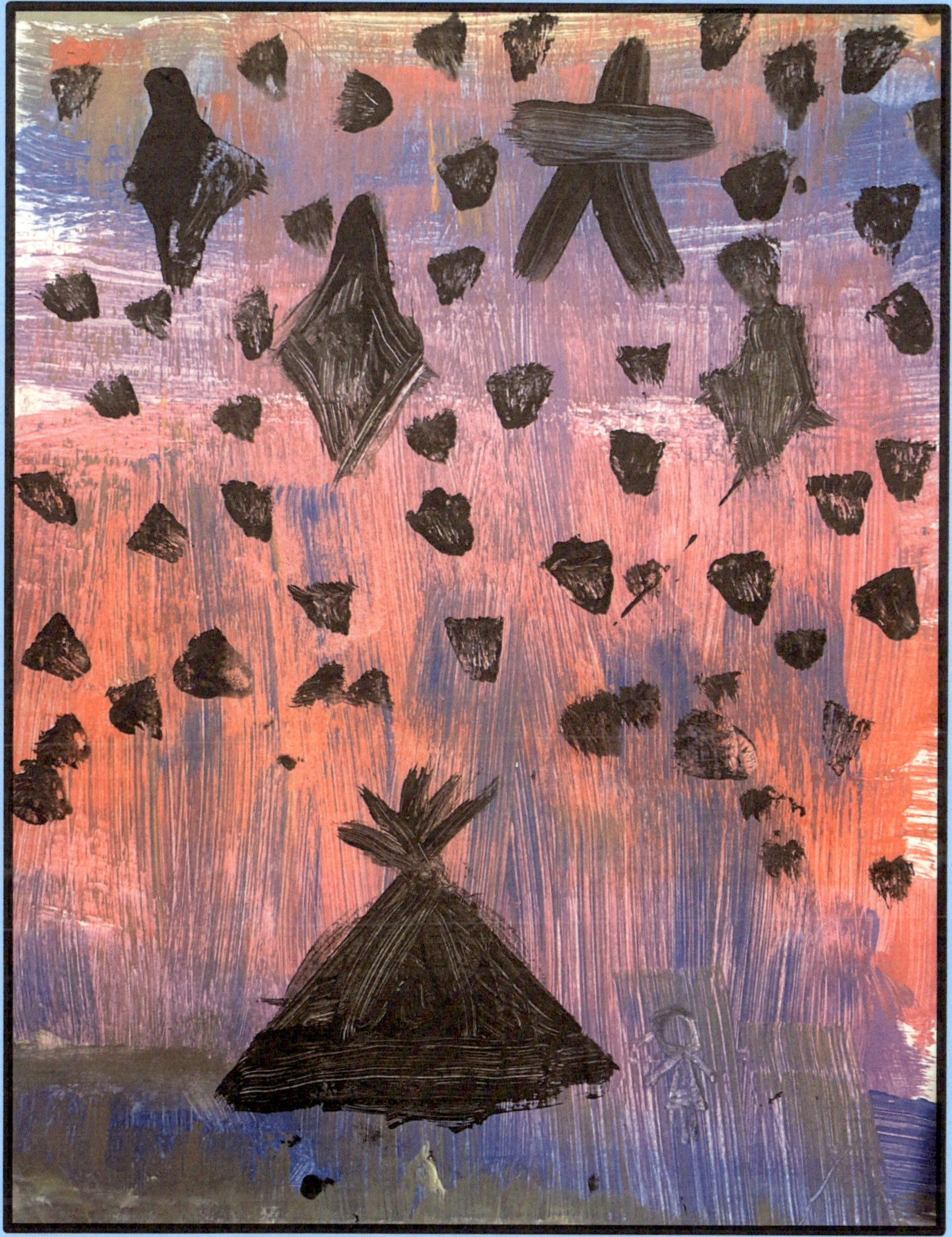

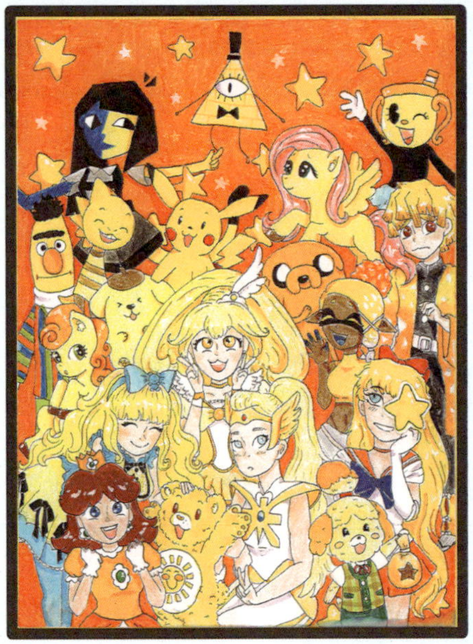
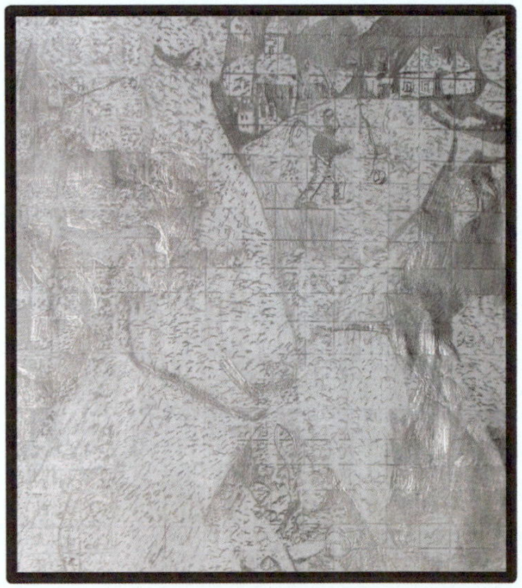
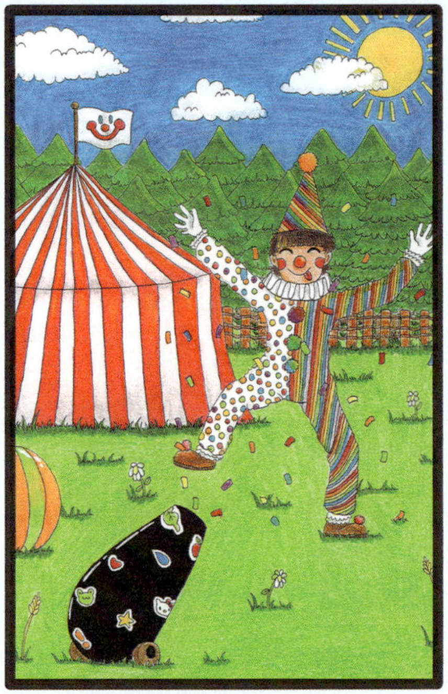
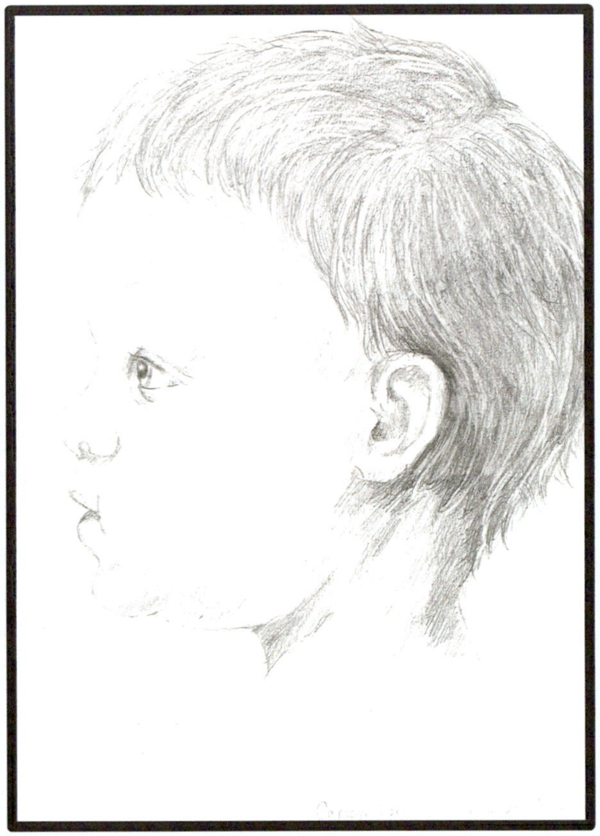
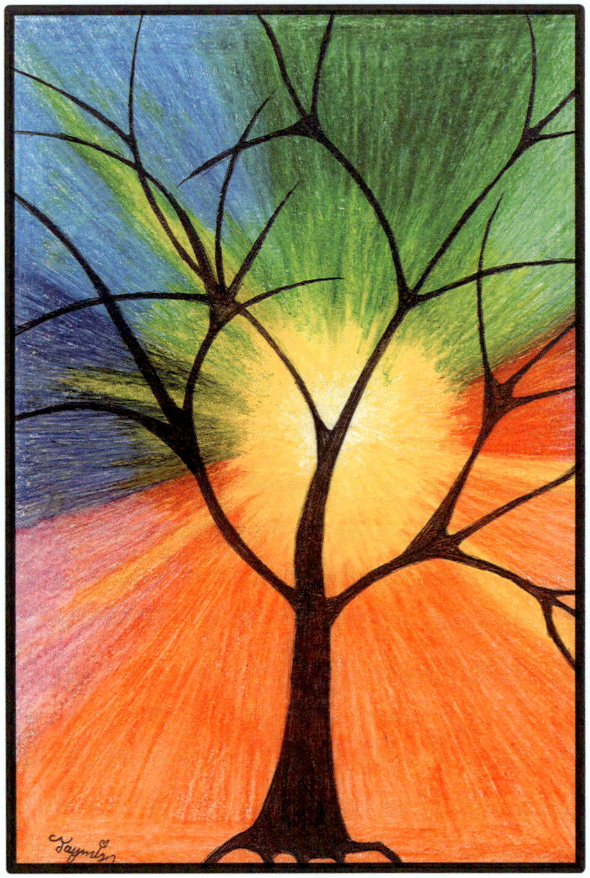
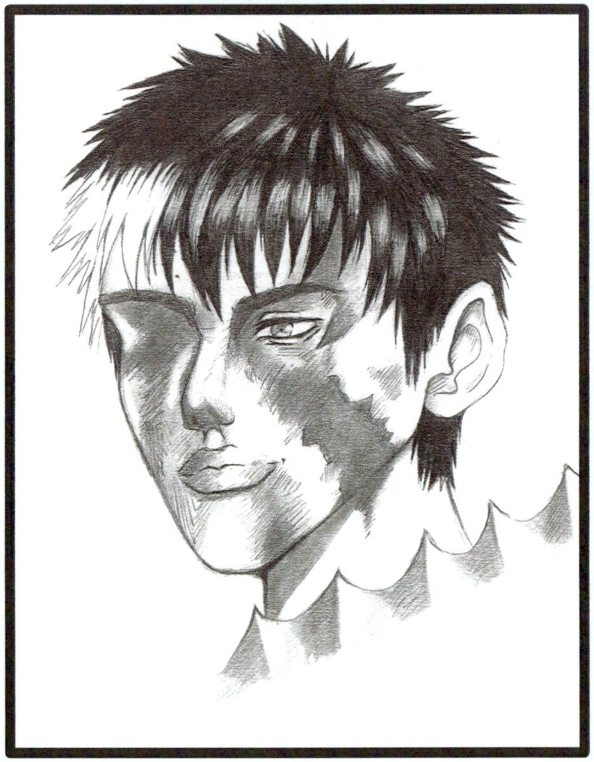

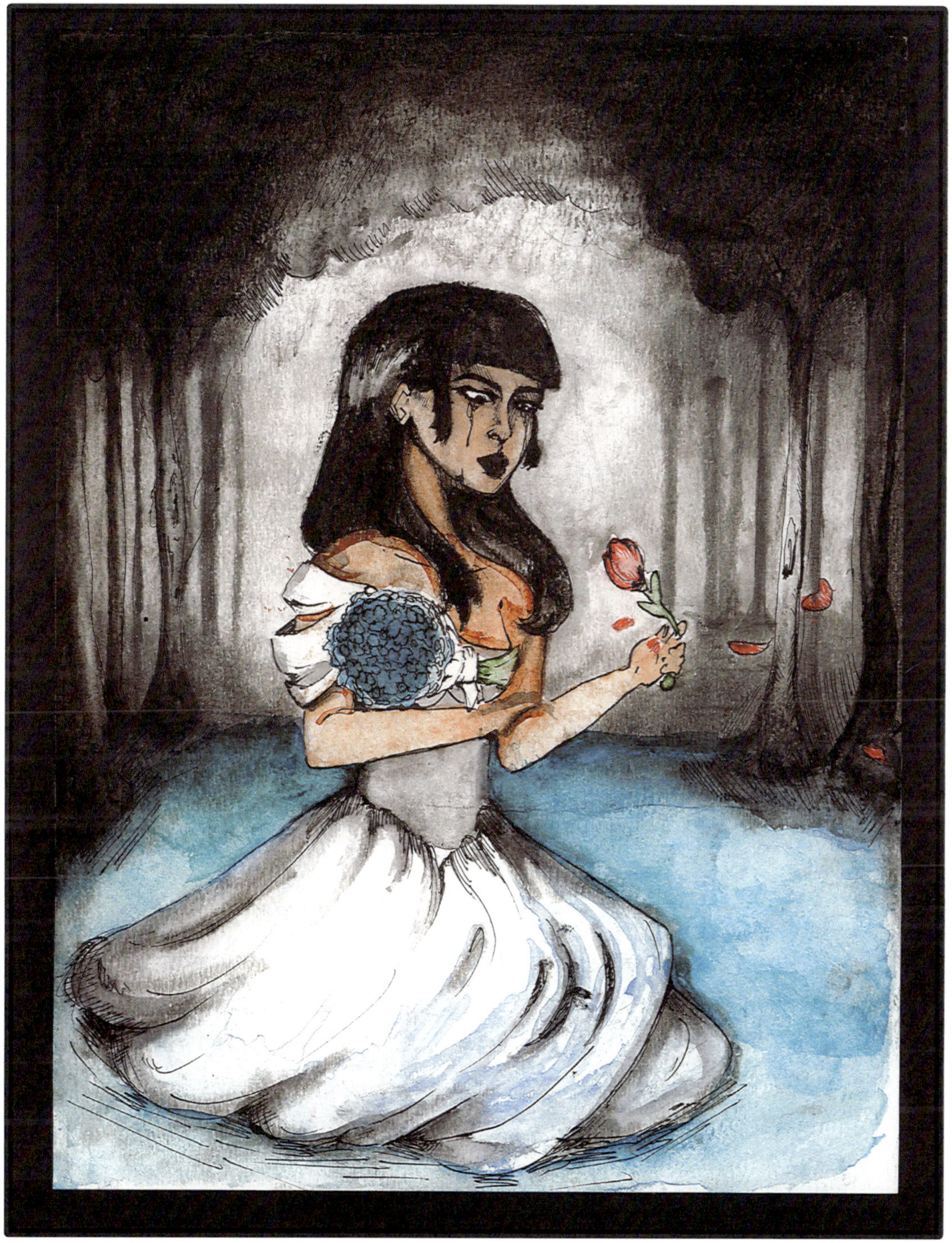

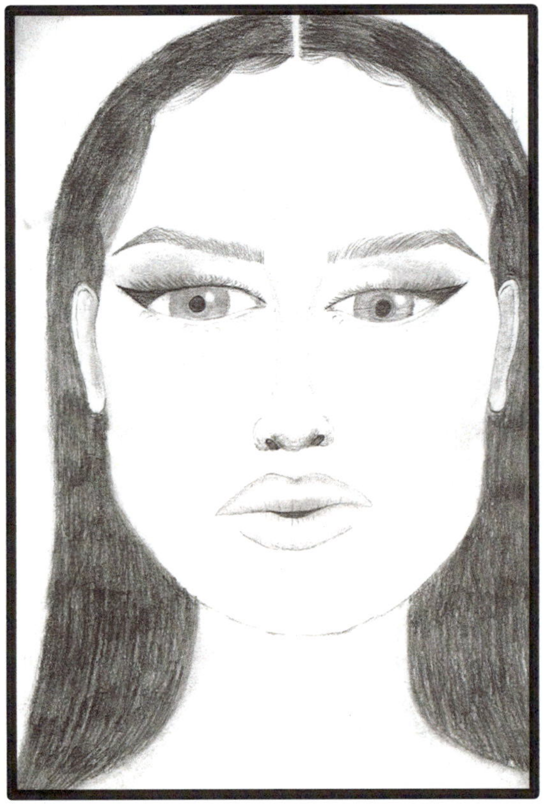

Ēkōma ēkwa ē-wāhpahcikātēki ēyikohk ōhi osīhcikēwin-iwa. Kiskinwahamawākanak ē-nihtā-kaskihocik. Ōki kistapinānih kihci-wiyasiwēwinahk ka-pimipayihtākik tānsi ka-ispayikowcik okiskinwahamawākanēyiwa.

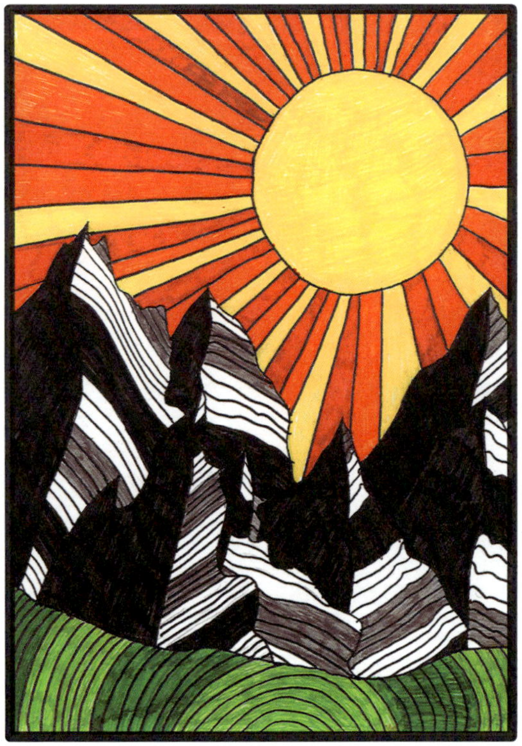

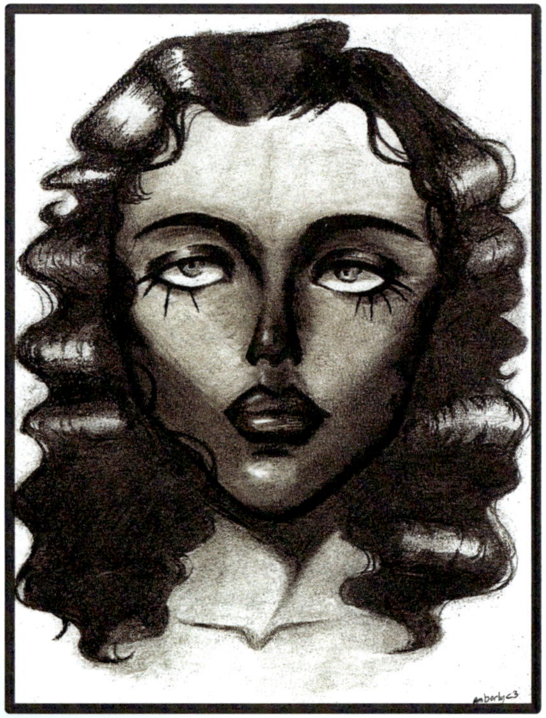

As one can see, there is a multitude of artistic talents that PAGC students possess.

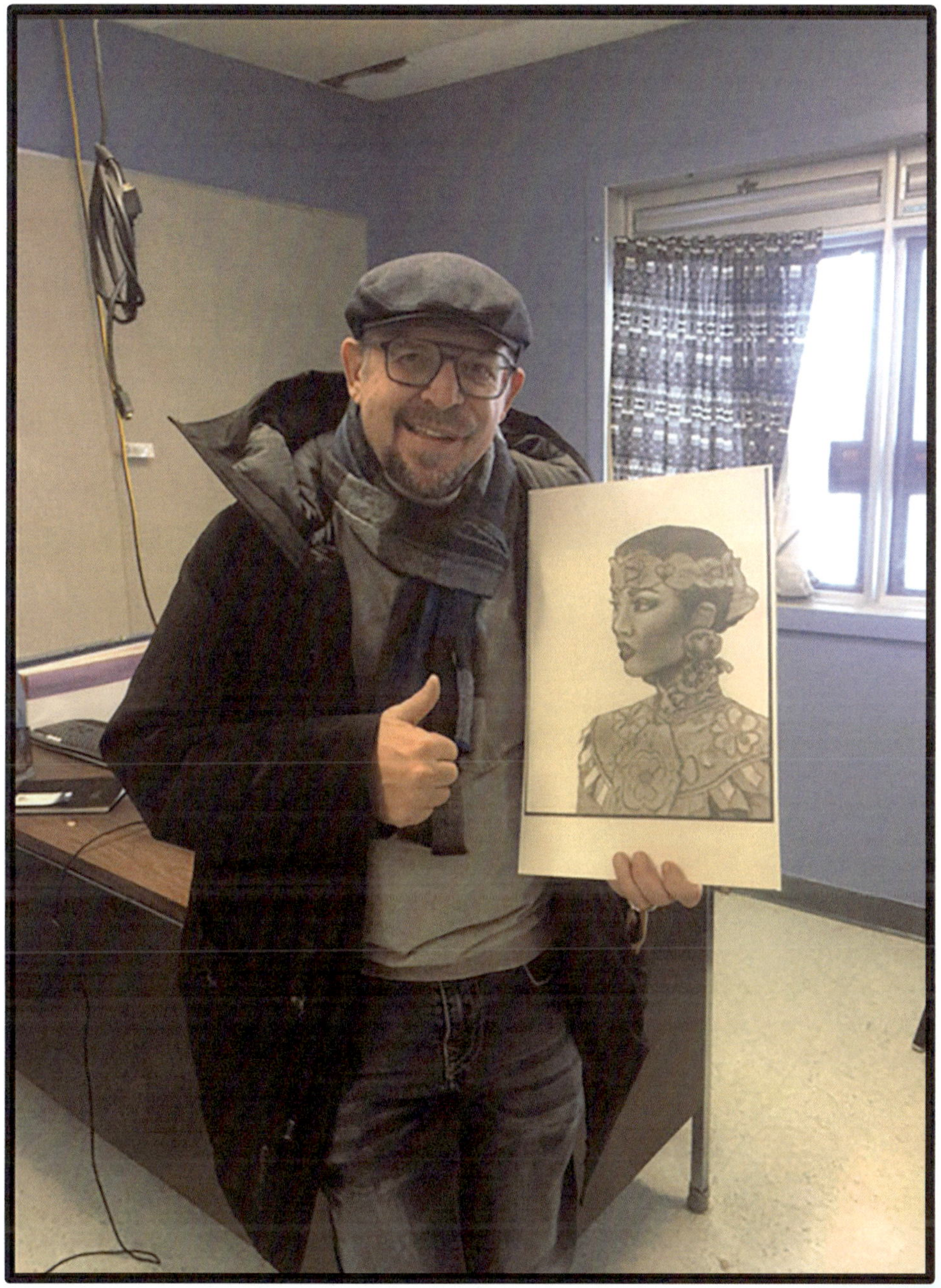

Kihci-osōniskwātahikēw theoren fleury pē-kiyokawēw gintautas sabaliauskawa kiskinwahamātowikamikosihk ē-pē-kanawāpahtak ōhi otāpasinahikēwiniya okiskinwahamawākana ka-osīhtāyit.

NHL Player, Theoren Fleury in Gintautas Sabaliauskas' classroom with his student's artwork.

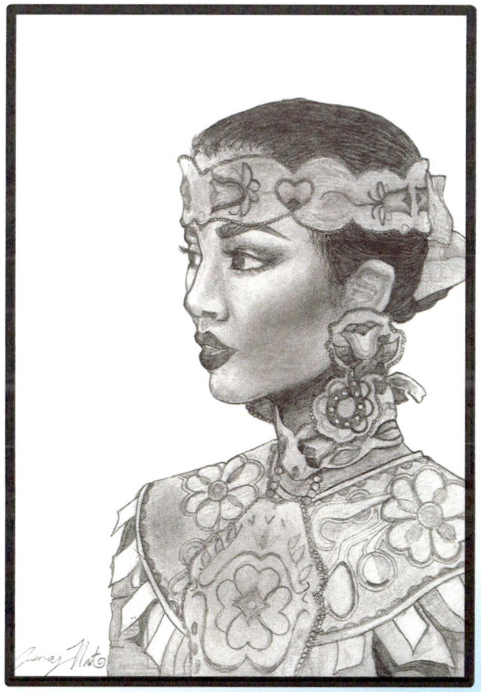

Oskinīkiskwēw crenay natomogan otasinahikēwin

Native Girl: Pencil drawing by Crenay Natomogan

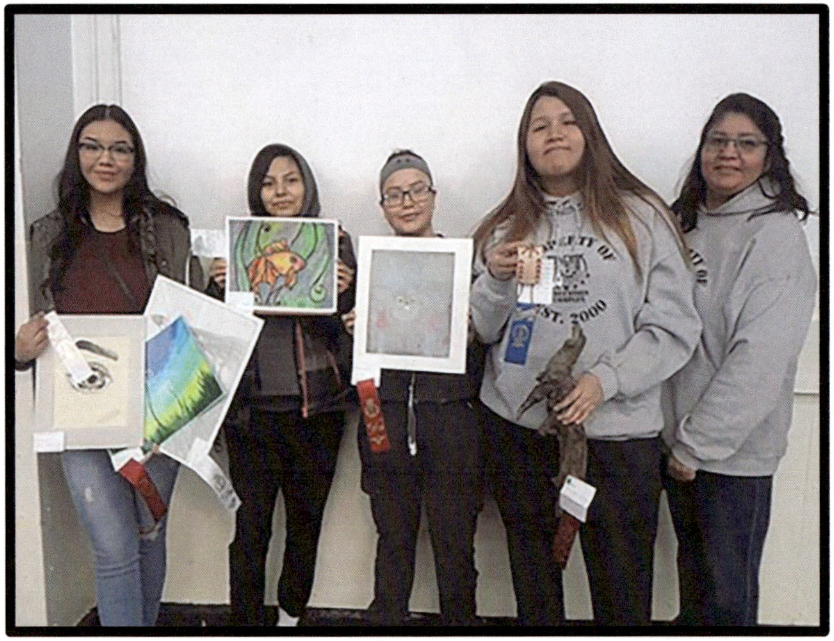

Tāpasinahikēwi-kiskinwahamākēwak kaskihtāwak ka-wīcihacik okishinwahamawākaniyiwa ka-nahtā-ayisiyiniwicik ōma ka-kiskinwahamākēcik ka-māmitonēyihcikēcik osīhcikēwinayiwa.

Art teachers can help students become more well-rounded and capable individuals by teaching them to develop original ideas through creative projects and practices.

Pāhkwāw sākahikanihk kiskinwahamākanak ohtinamok nīsitanaw-nēwosāp. Pīwāpiskāwa ōtē awasi-mōcikihtāwinihkēwin./ Shoal Lake students who received 24 medals at the last Fine Arts Festival.

Kistapinānihk kihci-wiyasiwēwak ka-pimipayihtācik nistawēyihcikātēw ōma ka-mamihcitotakosicik ōki kiskinwahamākēwak ka-miskwēyihtamipayiwa okinkinwahamākosowak ka-mi-yo-pimācihocik.

PAGC recognizes those teachers who inspire students' creativity in a positive and cultural way.

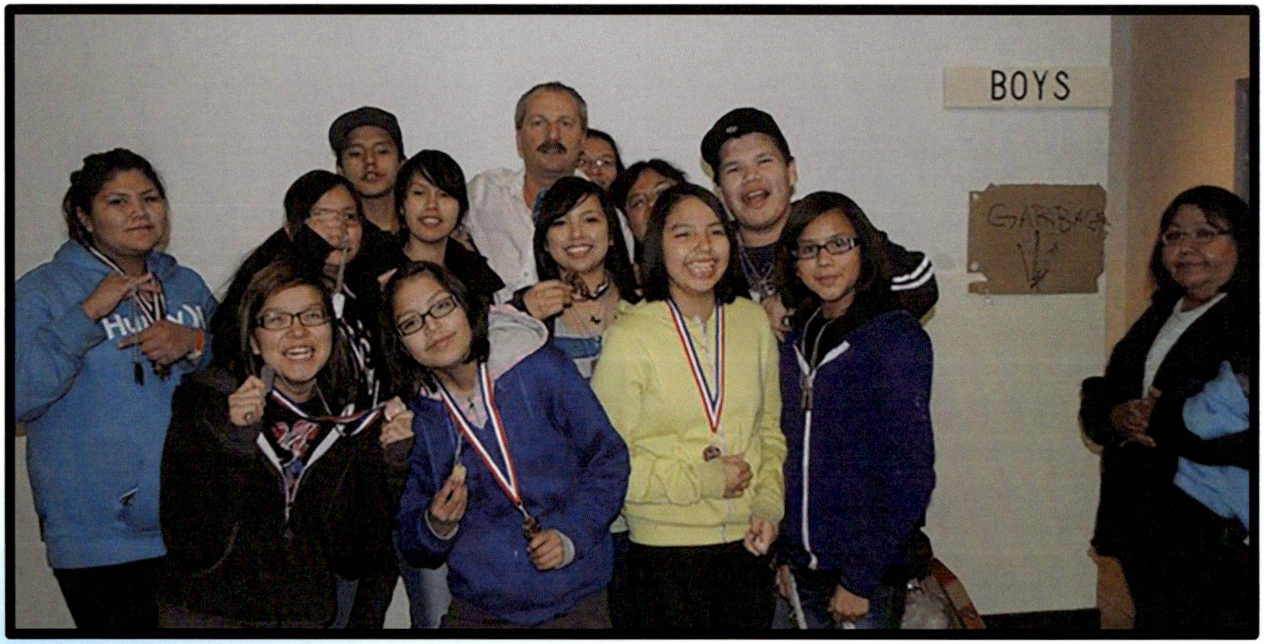

Pāhkwāw sākahikanihk mister sabaliauskas (nāwayikāpawiw) ē-wīci-nīpawīstamawācik ōhi awa nīkān ōtē okimāhkaniskwēw norma bear (kihciniskēhk)./Shoal Lake students Division 3-4 pose with their Art teacher, Mr. Sabaliauskas (middle back), and future chief Norma Bear (right).

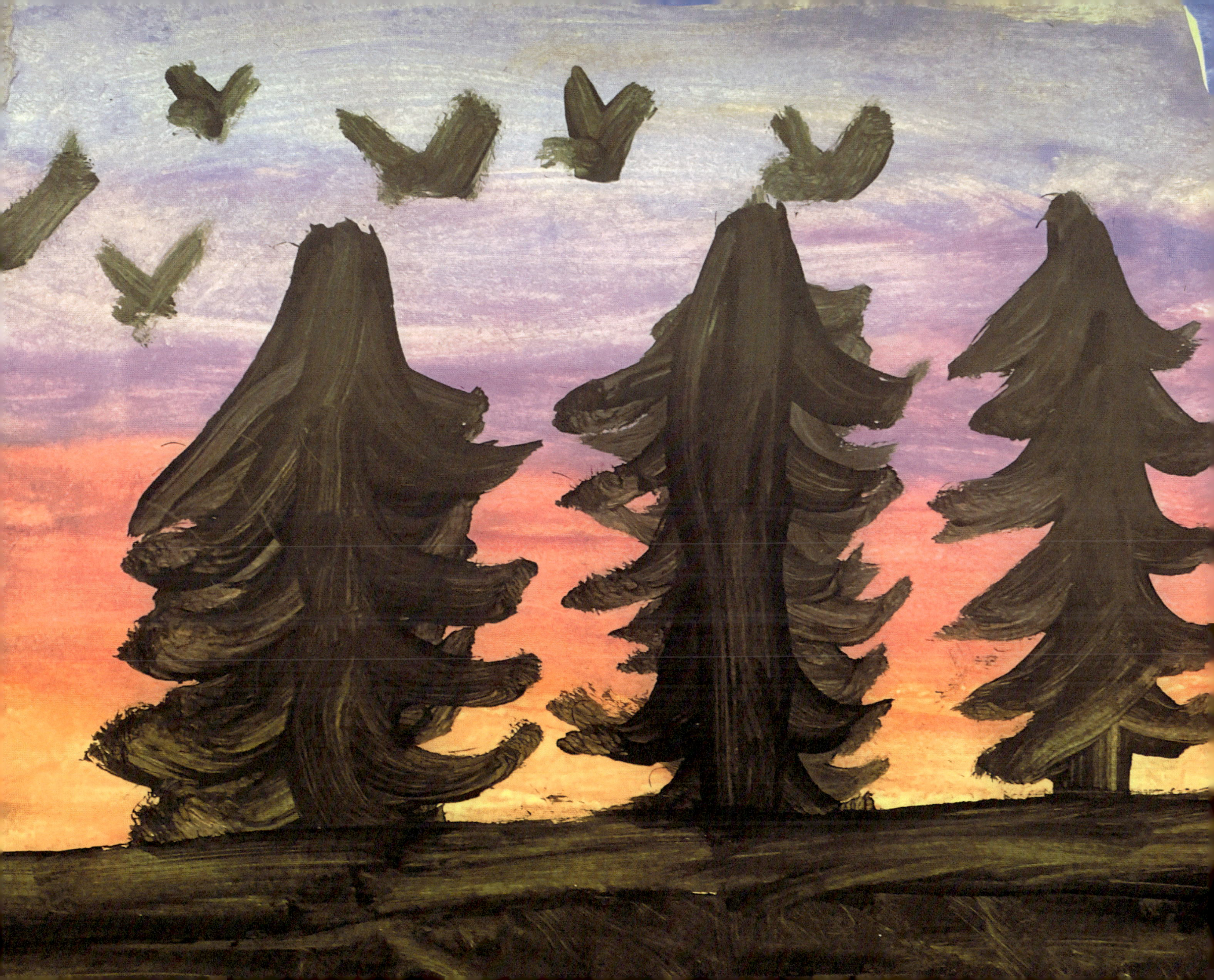

Memekwesiwuk (little People)

The little people were known to be powerful medicine men. They lived in caves along rocky shores. The elders offered tobacco when they saw little people. They also put tobacco in the cracks of the rock shore line. With tobacco offerings it was certain that they would get calm waters for their journey.

In the old days the little people would usully steal fish from the peoples nets, but at all same time would cut up nets and ruin them causing more work then needed. This happened to an old man who was angry at the little people. One night he paddled his canoe out on the lake where he set his nets.

He saw the little people coming out of the caves in their canoe and allowed them to approach the nets. He put his canoe between the caves and nets and waited. When the little people came back with a load of fish the old man grabbed the bow of their canoe and made the little people fall to the bottom of their canoe because they were ashamed of their faces. They didn't want to show the old man their faces because they were missing their noses. The reason the old man was there in the first place was that he didn't mind the little people taking fish from his nets. "It is just when you cut my nets, it takes many days to repare and my children go hungry," The little people were very sorry for causing the old man hardship. All the old man wanted was the promise that the little people won't cut up the fish nets again.

The two medicine men made a promise that they would never again cut up his nets the old man then let go of their canoe and made their way toward the cave. They paddled so fast the bounced off the cave becaus it had touched it the medicine men tourned their canoe around in attempted to try again and this time they disappeared into the cave. The old man never never had trouble with his nets again.

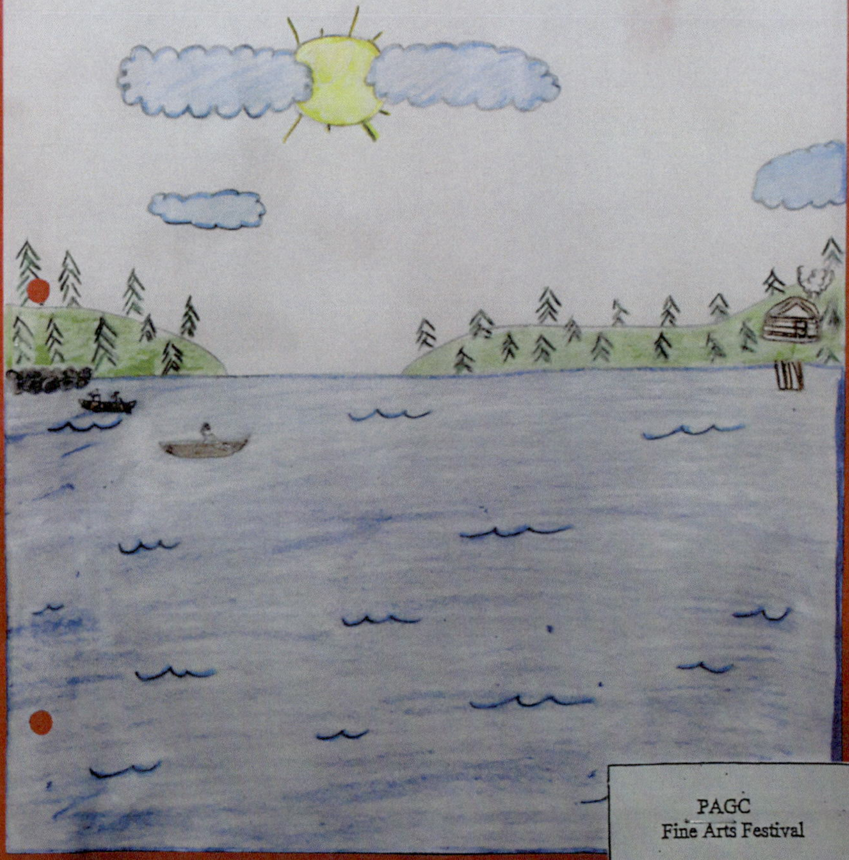

PAGC
Fine Arts Festival

Area: Literature
Category: Legends

Turning to traditions

What I think of the theme "Turning to traditions" is to talk to someone when you have a drug problem. Some of the people you could talk to are the guidance counselor's, elders, parents or someone you trust.

Alcohol is a killer. Alcohol destroys the liver, and does kill people. Alcohol disrupts towns and communities. Alcohol is a drug that some people turn to when they are trying to deal with a problem. It does not help at all but the only thing it does is makes the problem worse.

A lot of teens drink today because they think it is cool to drink. But the only thing cool about it is nothing. When they black out and don't know what is happening, they might make their selves look like fools or end up getting beaten. Sometimes they don't even know it happened. This is not a funny deal and some of the teens might try to commit suicide. The cause of teen drinking might be because they grew watching their parents drink.

A lot of parents drink because it is an addiction. It also might be because of the residential school syndrome. They want to try forget what happened to them while they were in the residential school. Alcohol is the reason I never got to see any of my grandfathers and this bothers me because I would have enjoyed their company.

Stanley mission is a dry reserve so if you get caught drinking in the reserve you will probably get charged or spend a night in the drunk tank.

Mark Mckenzie, kēka-mitātaht kapahisotahēt, nēwosāp ē-ispīhtisīt, ē-otahowēt ōma omasinahikēwin. "Kwēskī nēhiyawātisiwin isi" ē-isiyihkātēk."

Winning Essay entitled "Turning to Traditions"
by Mark McKenzie
Grade 9 Age 14

KAYĀSI-ĀCIKĀSTĒPICIKANA

PICTURES FROM THE PAST...

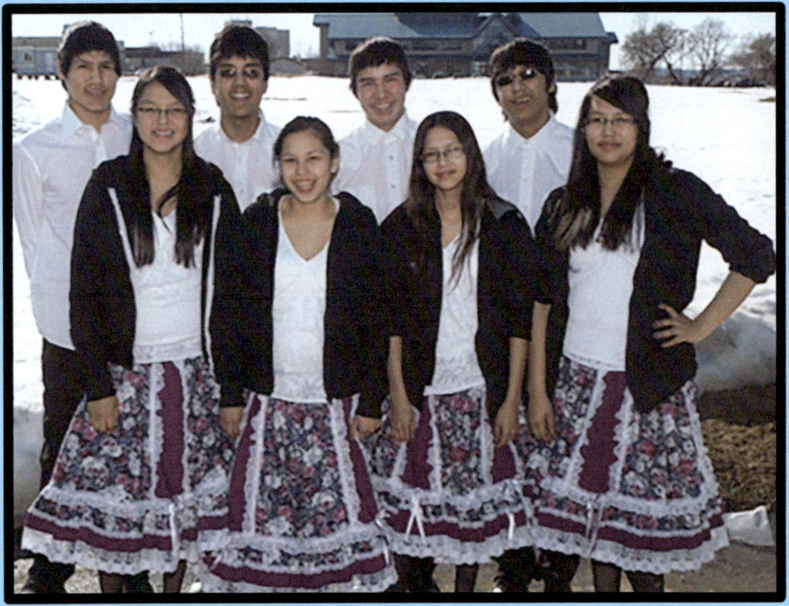

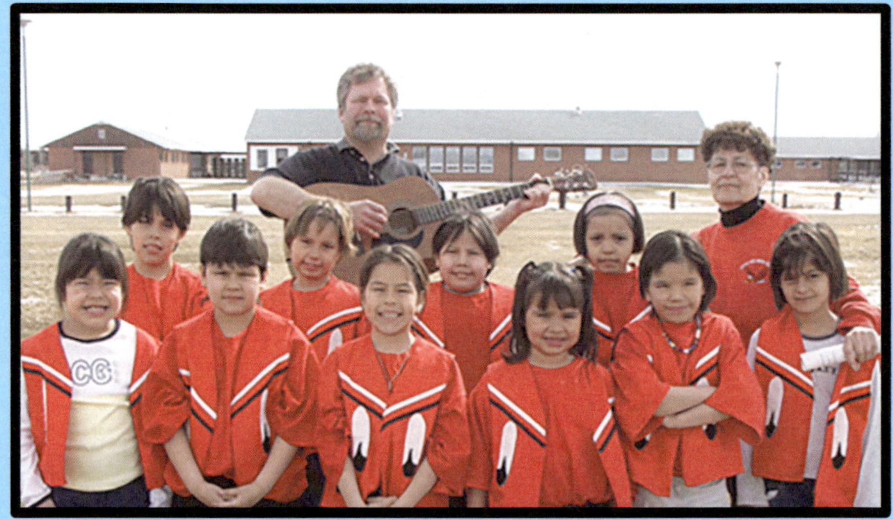

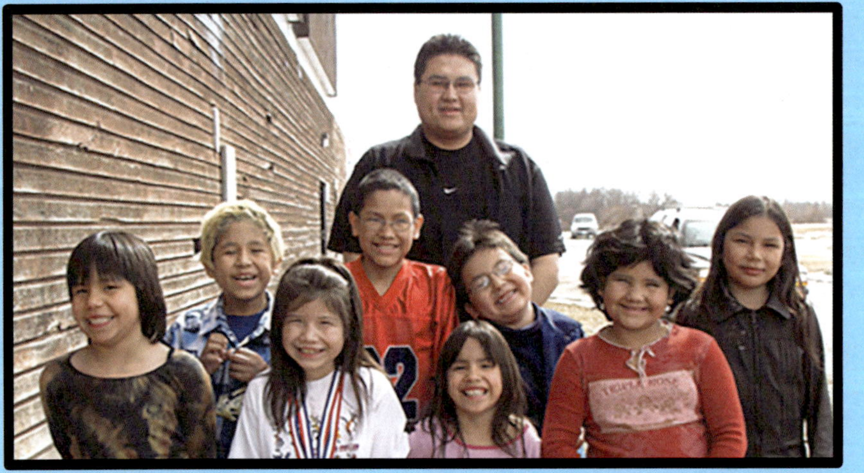

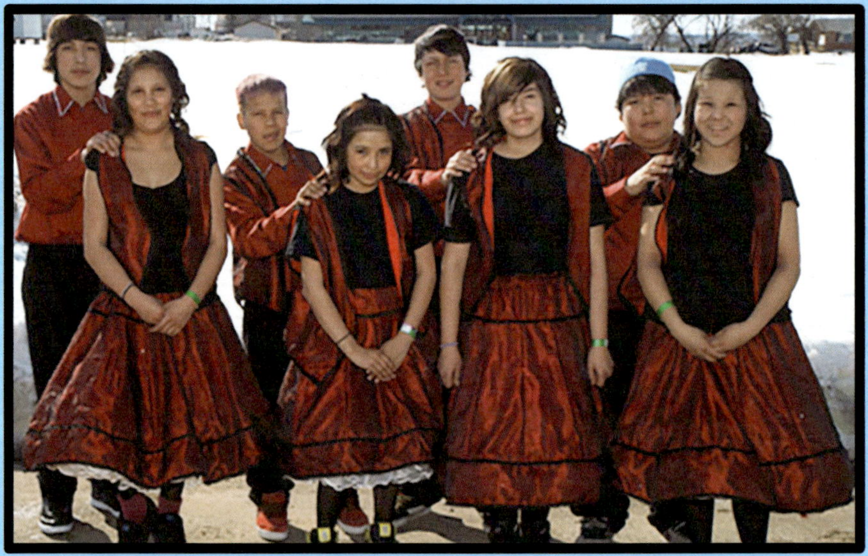

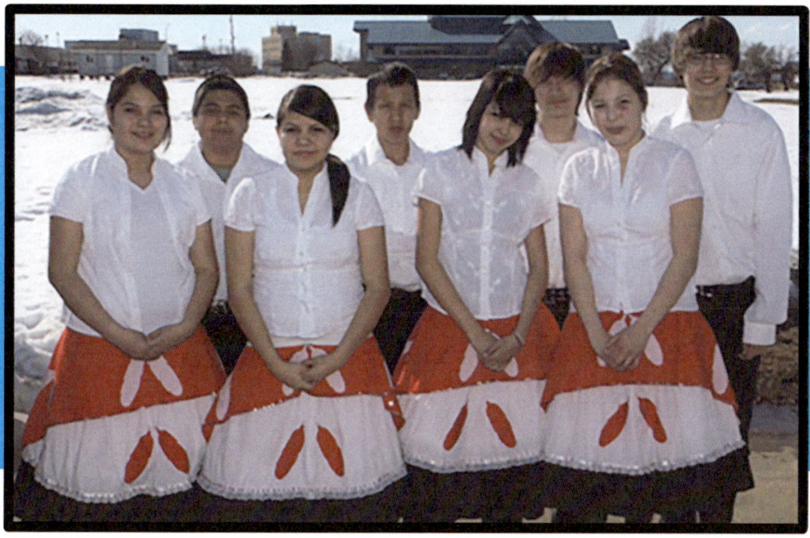

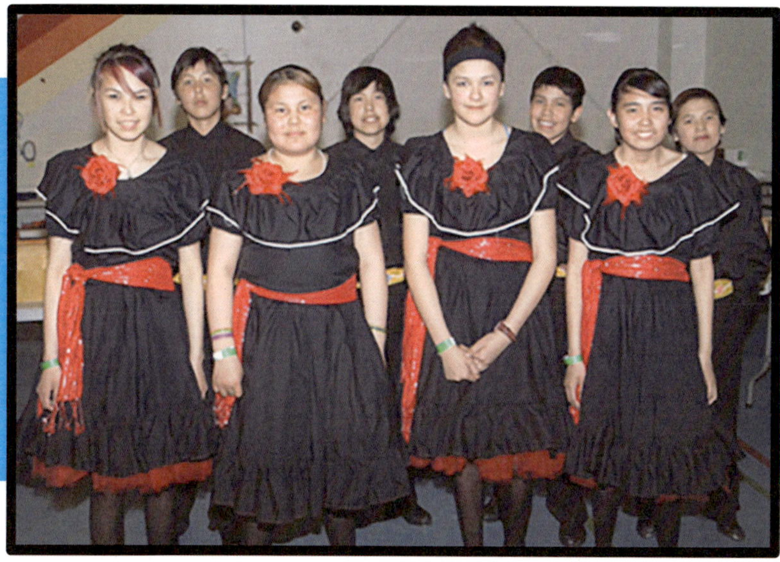

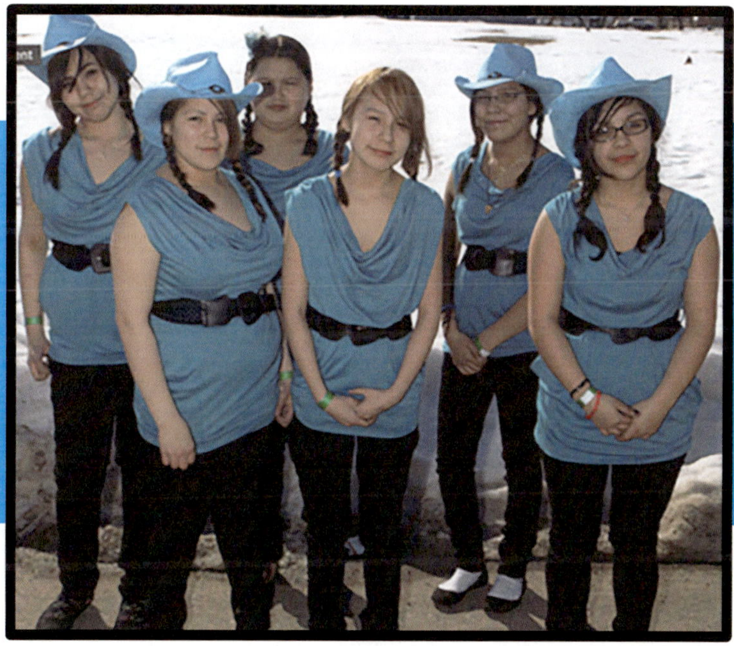

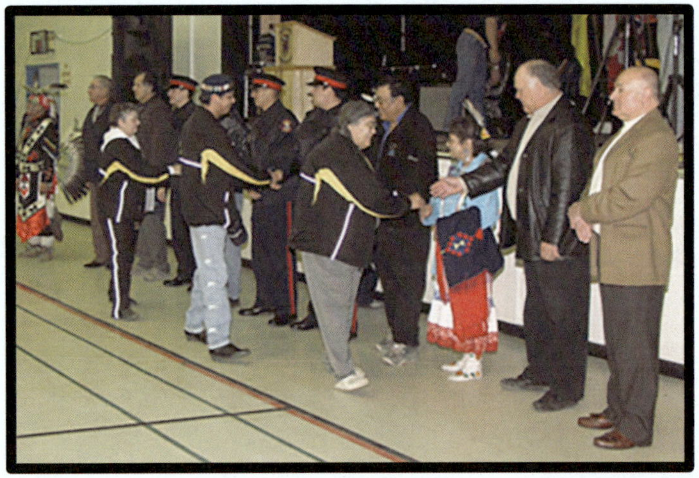

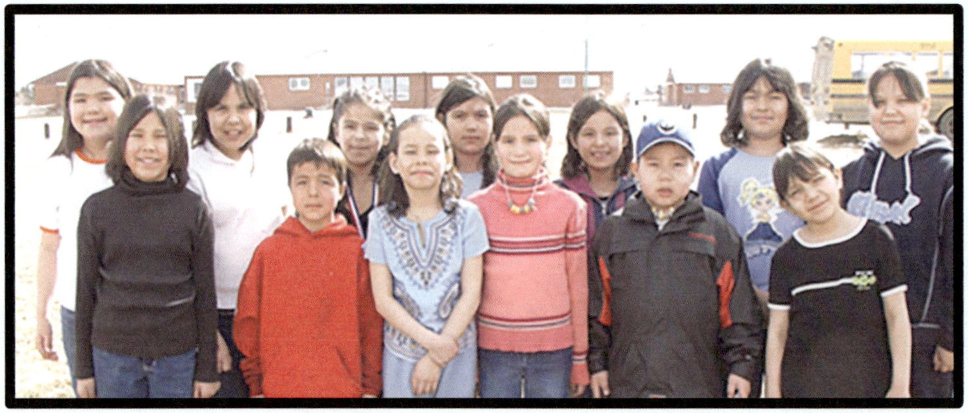

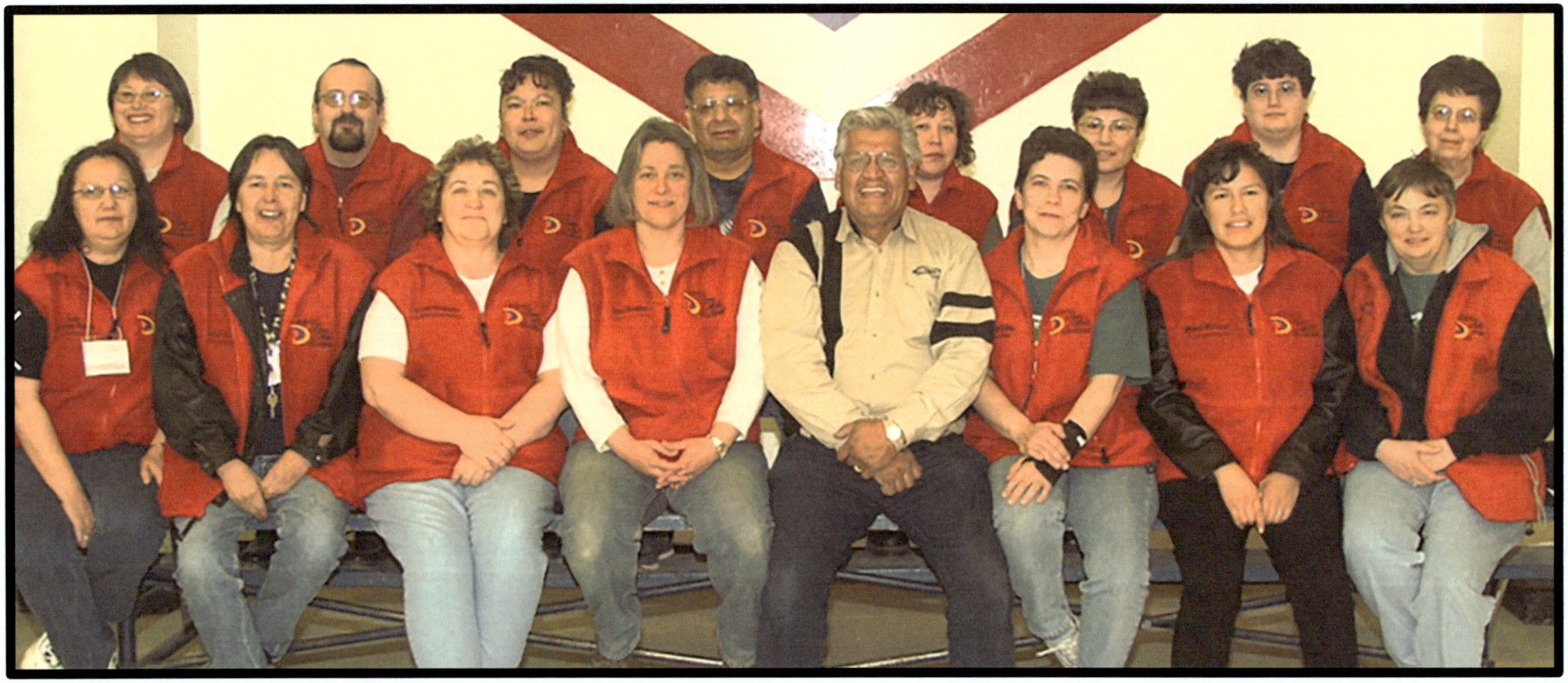

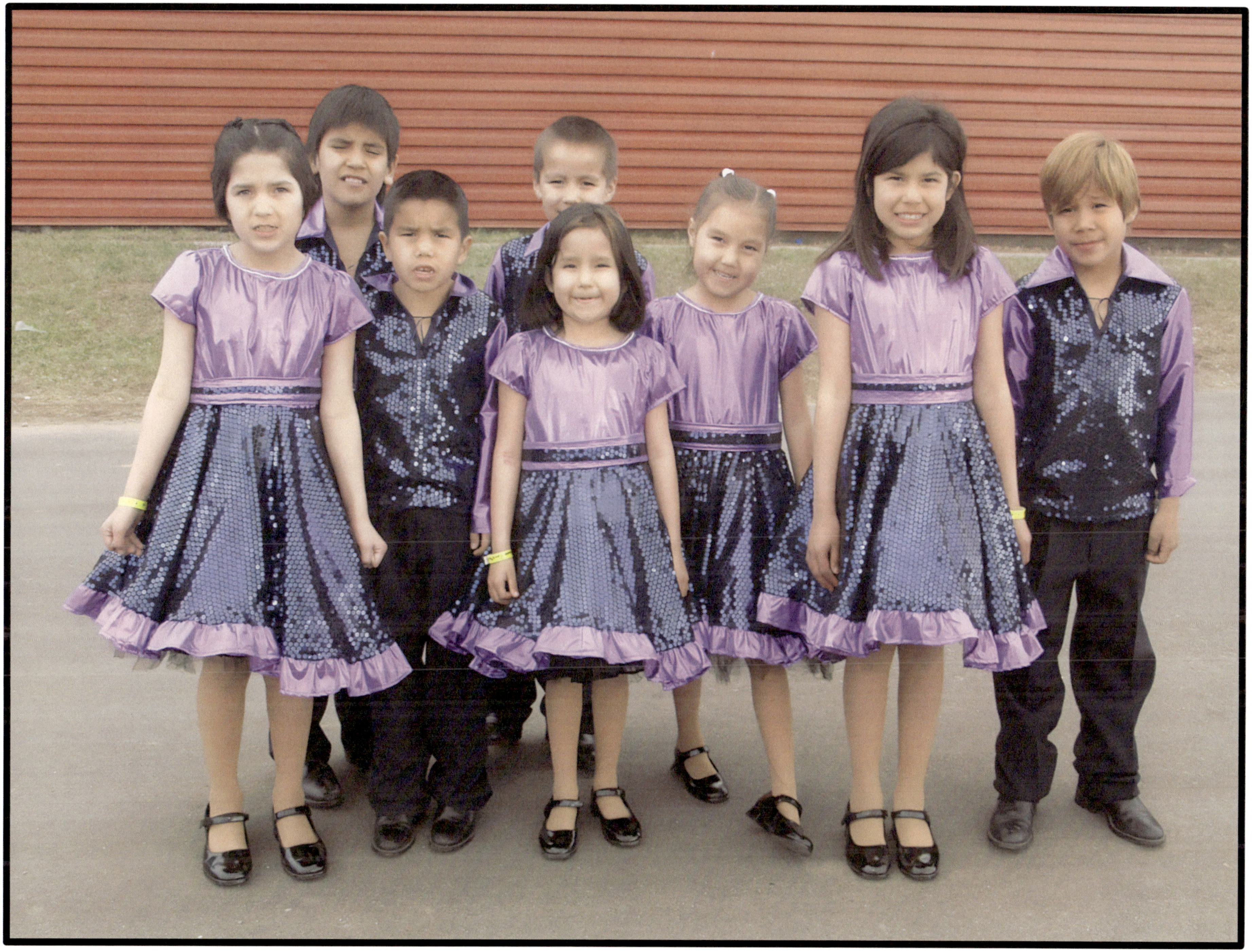

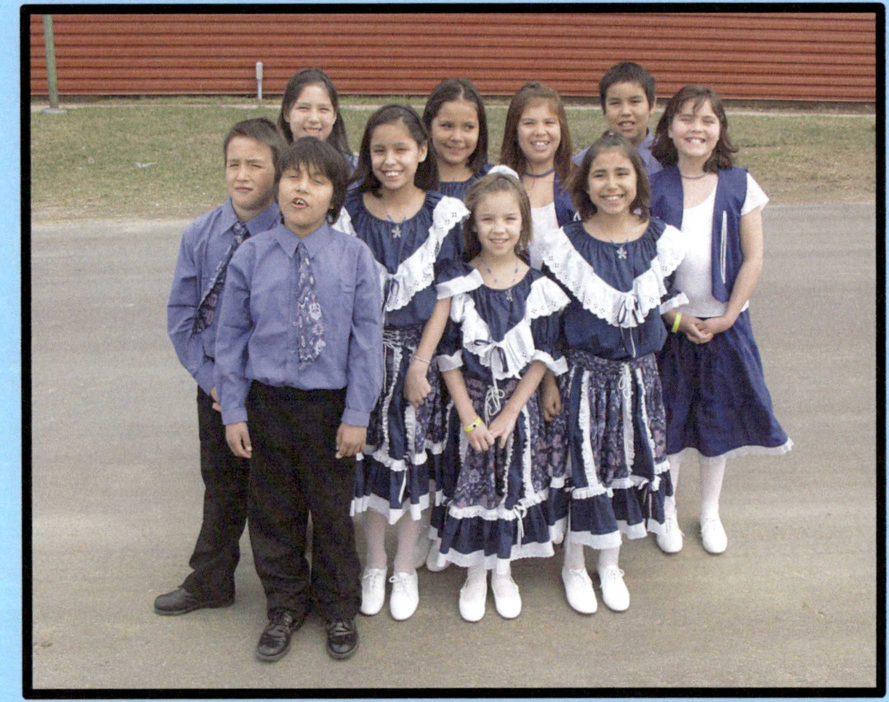

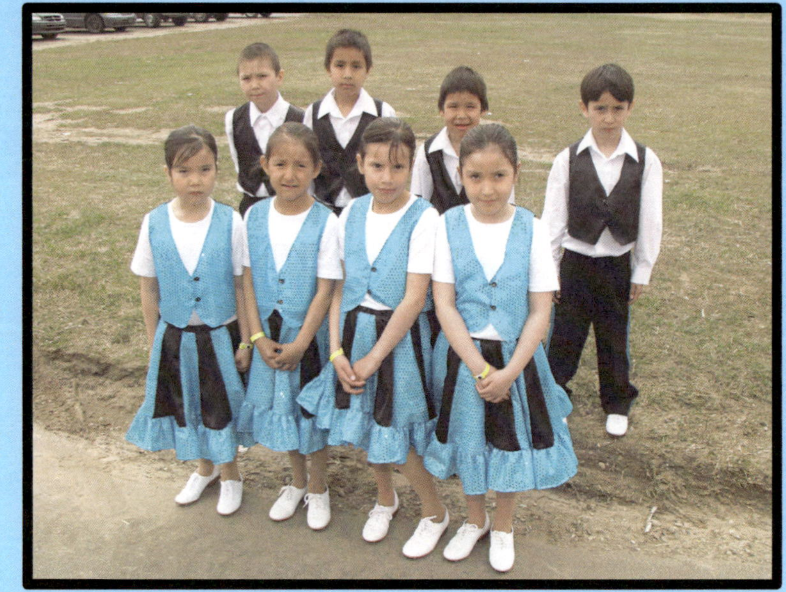

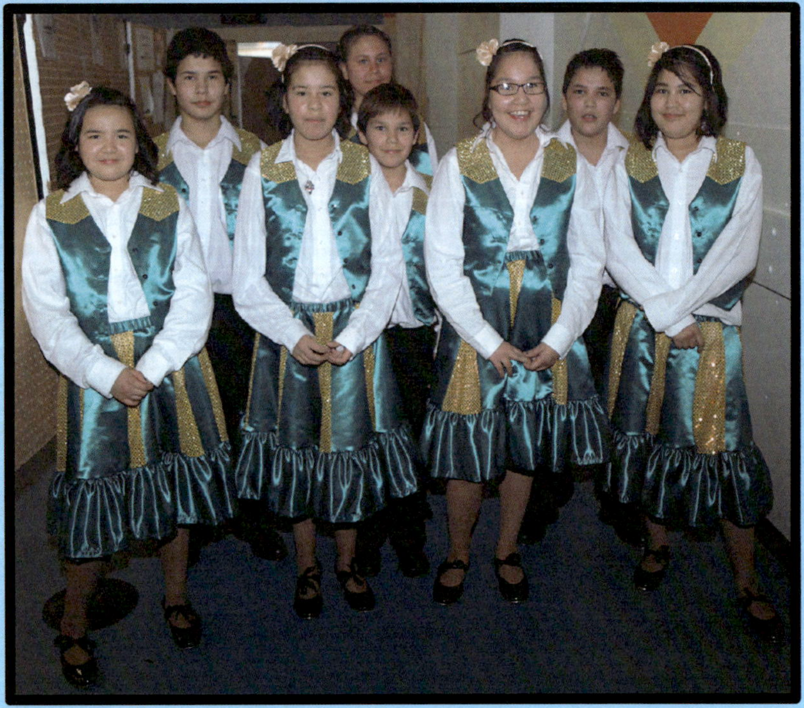

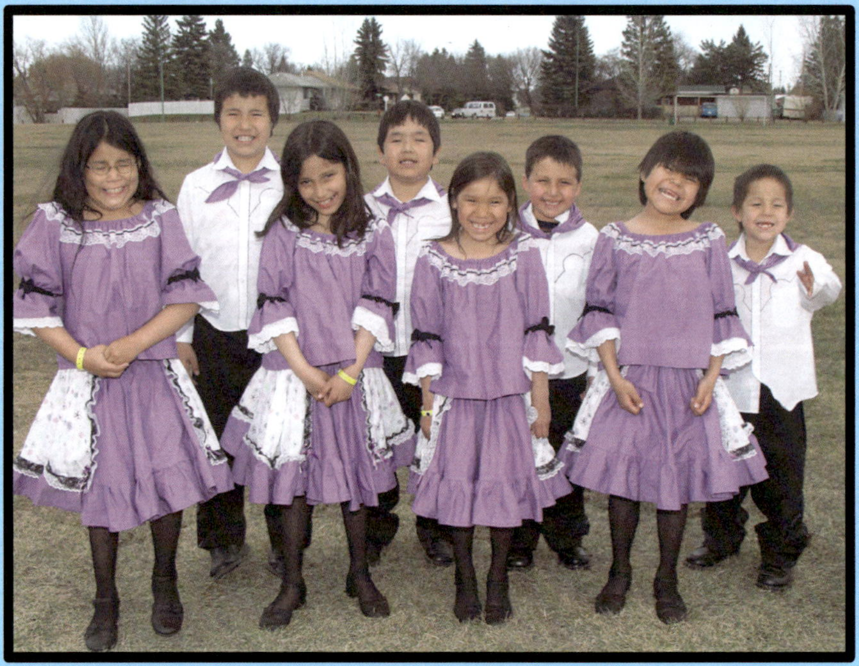

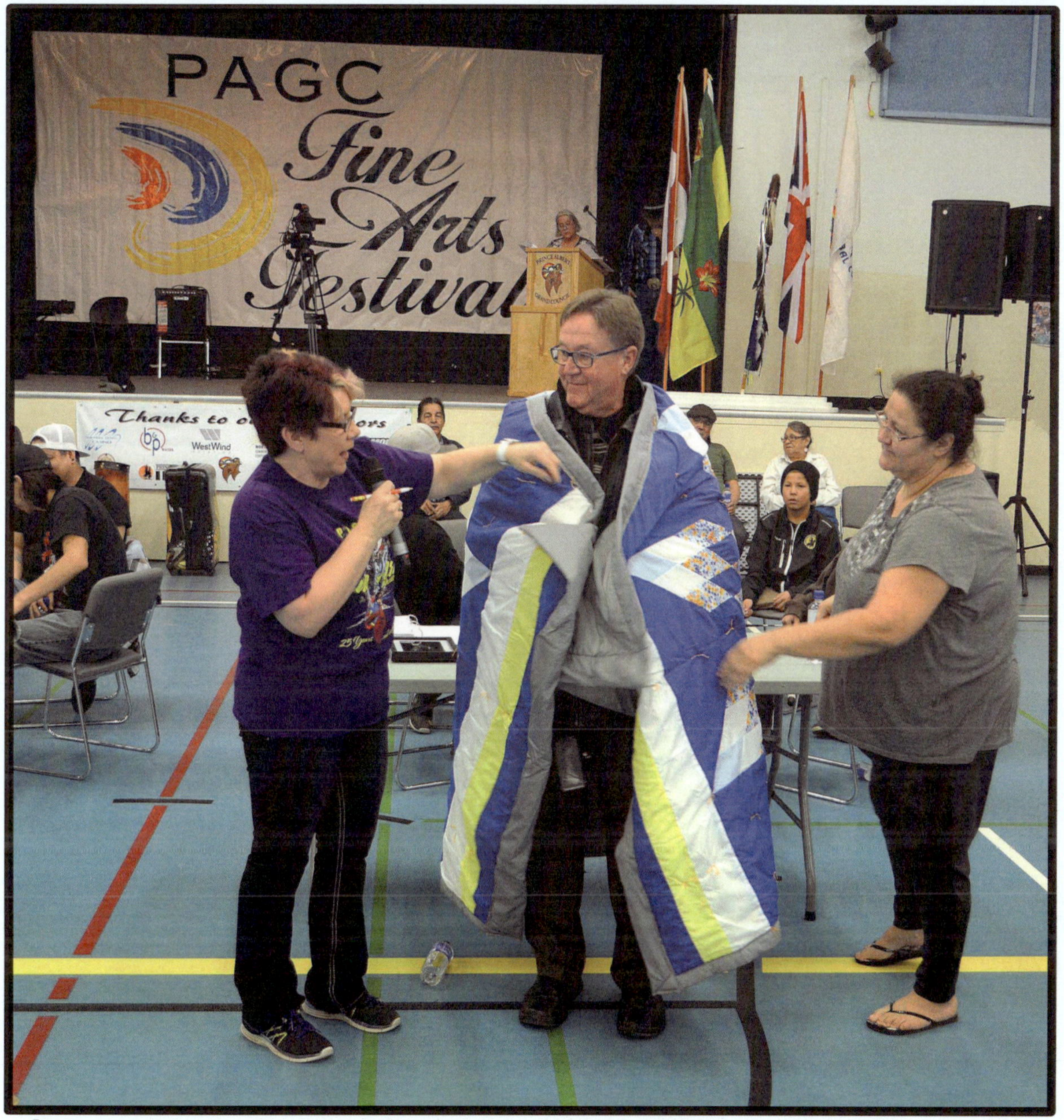

Ēkwāwa nāpēw, derroll lablanc kakī-mācihtāt mōcikihtāwinihkēwin ē-miyhīt atāhkakohp ēkota kistapinānihk kihci-wiyasiwēwak ōki kakī-pimipayihtācik kamōcikihtāwinihkēhk.

Derroll LeBlanc, the man who initially came up with the idea for the PAGC Fine Arts Festival, is presented with a star blanket at the PAGC Fine Arts Festival.

Acknowledgments

This is our 30th year! Such an event as large as the Festival cannot be done by just one or two people… It takes a large committee to help take on the many tasks. Thank you to all of you for taking the time to work with the committee. In most cases, it turns out to be so much more than sitting on a committee. Over the past 30 years we have seen many people come and go. They are all committed to one thing – making sure that their students and communities are involved in as much of the festival as possible. Whether it be recruiting the students to sign up for each of the events, collecting the artwork, crafts, and the literary pieces, recruiting other teachers to help in judging or chaperoning, gathering community members to help with the sewing of some of the costumes, organizing a mini festival or coaching the groups, all were dedicated to making it happen. This is for all of them – past and present.

The Prince Albert Grand Council wish to thank the Indigenous Languages Act (ILA) for providing financial support for the creation of this book. The Fine Arts Festival was developed with many of the initiatives proposed by federal grant such as creating access to resources to deliver activities that incorporate Indigenous languages, individuals and groups engaged in activities that strengthen Indigenous languages; and individuals and groups engaged as an integral part of Canadian society, and embrace and share their languages with other Canadians.

This event would not take place without the full support of the communities, the schools, the Education Directors and of course, the leadership. We are grateful that this event has continued to garner support from the leadership as well as the community and the schools. To the leadership, we are eternally grateful for your support and encouragement. Our leadership, which includes all the First Nation Chiefs as well as the Chiefs and Executive at the Prince Albert Grand Council, continues to support the Festival and agree that it is the best event that we host for the children. Thank you for your continued encouragement and support in making this festival a reality and helping it to grow over the past 30 years.

We say a special thank you to Ron Merasty of the PAGC Tribune for providing many of the photographs used in this book.

To the students...our artists...we thank you for your creativity and your willingness to share your talents at the Festival.

To everyone involved with making the Fine Arts Festival a reality we send you our thanks and eternal gratitude.